Food and Agriculture Organization of the United Nations

UNECE

# FOREST SECTOR OUTLOOK STUDY 2020-2040

UNITED NATIONS
Geneva, 2021

## COPYRIGHT AND DISCLAIMER



## ABSTRACT

The Forest Sector Outlook 2020-2040 study for the UNECE region provides information that supports decision-making by showing the possible medium- and long-term consequences of specific policy choices and structural changes, using scenario analyses whenever possible. The study is the first to cover the entire UNECE region and provides results for the main UNECE subregions of Europe, North America and the Russian Federation.

The study provides insight on six priority questions which were identified through a transparent and participatory process: (i) *How would different demand changes affect the UNECE forest products market?*; (ii) *How would different supply changes affect the UNECE region forest products markets?* (iii) *How would significant trade restrictions affect the UNECE region forest product markets?* (iv) *How will UNECE forests be affected by climate change?* (v) *How could UNECE region forests and the forest sector contribute to climate change mitigation?* (vi) *How could UNECE forests adapt to climate change?*

The study contains information on the possible impacts of future trends regarding the future forest carbon sink in tonnes of $CO_2$ equivalents, and on harvest, production, consumption, net exports and prices of wood products by 2040.The study takes a pragmatic, transparent and objective approach to answering these key questions, sometimes using a modelling approach. It enables stakeholders to evaluate the long-term consequences of policy choices.

The study contributes to evidence-based policy formulation and decision making. It is not a forecast of what will happen in the future. Rather, it sheds light on the possible consequences of policy choices and of factors external to the forest sector, most notably anthropogenic climate change. The study draws attention to the following issues emerging from the analysis in the study, and asks questions which policy makers and stakeholders might consider: (i) *Disturbances and the forest sink*; (ii) *Demand for land for increased carbon sequestration by forests*; (iii) *Putting substitution in a wider context*; (iv) *Trade measures*, and; (v) *Need for a system-wide, holistic approach to strategies and policies.*

ECE/TIM/SP/51

UNITED NATIONS PUBLICATION

**Sales No.** E.22.II.E.11

**ISBN** 978-92-1-117289-8

**eISBN** 978-92-1-001297-3

**ISSN** 1020-2269

**eISSN** 2518-6450

## FOREWORD

Forests are an integral part of our future. The planetary health and the livelihoods of 1.6 billion people worldwide are directly linked to forests. The COVID -19 pandemic has taught us to re-discover and value our forests' contribution to our health, well-being and to sustainable development. Forests are key to climate change mitigation. Their potential as a natural carbon sink is essential to stabilize greenhouse gas emissions and to tackle global warming. Forests are crucial for preventing natural disasters and building resilience for our citizens.

Forests also need to quickly adapt to changing climatic conditions since they are particularly vulnerable to climate induced impacts and to adverse land use and production choices. Governments and societies are currently focusing on the short- and medium-term fallouts of the COVID-19 pandemic and the global disruptions in the forest-based supply chains. In the meantime, more powerful, long-term tectonic shifts are under way, changing the economic, social and environmental situation worldwide. Climate change, an increasing global population and the geographical shifting of the global middle class are likely to unfold in complex ways that could inflict profound changes on production, trade and consumption globally.

These megatrends are expected to have significant impacts on forests and forest products in the UNECE region and globally. Global megatrends are outside the control of national policy makers, but they require increasingly complex choices at international, regional, national and local levels. This complexity calls for thorough global or regional assessments of their possible impacts in the coming years.

Member States of the UNECE region have a long track record of sustainably managing their forests while remaining the most significant wood product producers in the world. This new study is the latest in a series of Forest Sector Outlook Studies which have supported policy making since the first edition was published in 1952, aiming at assisting policy makers in this complex task now and in the future.

The study, including modelling and analyzing different scenarios, has been developed in collaboration with national and international partners. It points out issues that need further consideration to continue sustainable forest management in the UNECE region in the decades to come. It also offers food for thought to guide decisions on complex trade-offs facing policymakers and forest managers in light of climate change and changing demographics.

We would like to express our sincere gratitude to all partners who have contributed to this comprehensive, new and innovative Forest Sector Outlook Study which we hope will help sustainably manage the future of forests.

**Olga ALGAYEROVA**
Under-Secretary-General of the United Nations,
Executive Secretary of the United Nations
Economic Commission for Europe

**Vladimir RAKHMANIN**
Assistant Director-General,
Regional Representative for Europe and Central Asia of the
Food and Agriculture Organization of the United Nations

# Contents

# List of tables



# List of figures



# List of boxes

## ACKNOWLEDGEMENTS

The UNECE/FAO Forestry and Timber Section expresses its deep gratitude to the contributors of this Forest Sector Outlook Study 2020-2040. The UNECE/FAO Forestry and Timber Section is grateful to the Netherlands and the Swiss Confederation for their financial support to the preparation of the study.

The study is the result of a cooperative effort involving a network of authors, reviewers, editors, the UNECE/FAO Team of Specialists on Forest Sector Outlook, and the Forestry and Timber Section team in Geneva as well as FAO in Rome. In combination, this network provides an unrivalled source of expertise and knowledge, which is the hallmark of this *Outlook Study* and previous editions

Many of those involved in producing the study volunteered their time and expertise; others are supported by administrations, universities, industry associations and various other organizations. Some of these in-kind contributions were particularly valuable for conceptualizing the study. The UNECE/FAO Forestry and Timber Section would like to express its gratitude to the European Forest Institute (EFI) and the EFI Network Fund project "Forest Management Scenarios for Adaptation and Mitigation" (FORMASAM), the German Academic Exchange Service and the Potsdam Institute for Climate Impact Research and Wageningen University and Research (in particular the Graduate School for Production Ecology and Resource Conservation and the knowledge base programme Circular and Climate Neutral Society) for their contribution to the analytical parts of this study. We also thank the United States Forest Service for their important contribution to the modelling and analytical work.

We acknowledge the following authors who wrote the chapters and, in so doing, shared their expertise and knowledge (contact details and affiliations of all authors are in the annex):

| Galina Churkina | Mariana Hassegawa | Tristan Herrmann | Louis König | Prakash Nepal |
|---|---|---|---|---|
| Jeffrey Prestemon | Christopher Prins | Christopher P.O. Reyer | Mart-Jan Schelhaas | Pieter Johannes Verkerk |

The UNECE/FAO Forestry and Timber Section expresses its appreciation to the contributing experts Elias Hurmekoski, John Kim, Ragnar Jonsson, Marcus Lindner and Gert-Jan Nabuurs for the information and assistance received in preparing the *Outlook Study*.

Special thanks to Christopher (Kit) Prins for his help as coordinating author in streamlining and finalizing the study.

Douglas Clark edited the publication.

The study was managed by the UNECE/FAO Forestry and Timber Section and reviewed by the FAO.

This manuscript was completed on 12 November 2021.


## EXPLANATORY NOTES

For ease of reading, the publication mostly provides value data in United States dollars (indicated by the sign "$" or as "dollars").

See the map in the annex for a breakdown of the region into its subregions. References to EU27 refer collectively to the 27 country members of the European Union. When "Europe" or "EU" is mentioned in connection with a reference, i.e. not as part of the modelling analysis, then it refers to the group of countries as defined by the reference. The term Eastern Europe, Caucasus and Central Asia (EECCA) is used for reasons of geographic proximity and similarities in economic structure and refers collectively to 12 countries: Armenia, Azerbaijan, Belarus, Georgia, Kazakhstan, Kyrgyzstan, Republic of Moldova, Russian Federation, Tajikistan, Turkmenistan, Ukraine and Uzbekistan. It is used solely for the reader's convenience.

The term industrial roundwood is used interchangeably with logs.

All references to tonnes in this text represent the metric unit of 1,000 kilograms unless otherwise indicated.

A billion refers to a thousand million ($10^9$). One trillion refers to one million million, or $10^{12}$.

Nonwood forest products are part of the broader concept of the provision of ecosystem services through forests. However, due to limitations in resources available and guidance received by member States and the necessity of focusing on the six questions identified at the beginning of the process. The study was not able to assess the impact of future trends on important services and products such as e.g. honey, medicinal plants, nuts, fruits, mushrooms, pollination, erosion prevention, etc. In some regions of the UNECE, these goods and services may even exceed the social and economic value of wood and wood products from forests.

# List of Acronyms and Abbreviations

| | |
|---|---|
| **$** | United States dollar(s) unless otherwise specified |
| **...** | unavailable |
| **AWC** | American Wood Council |
| **CBD** | Convention on Biological Diversity |
| **China-HWC** | China-High Wood Consumption |
| **CLT** | cross-laminated timber |
| **$CO_2$** | Carbon dioxide |
| **COFFI** | The UNECE Committee on Forests and the Forest Industry |
| **COVID-19** | coronavirus disease of 2019 |
| **CSF** | Climate-Smart Forestry |
| **EECCA** | Eastern Europe, Caucasus and Central Asia |
| **EFC** | European Forestry Commission |
| **EFI** | European Forest Institute |
| **EFSOS** | European Forest Sector Outlook Study |
| **ESG** | environmental social and governance |
| **ETTS** | European Timber Trend Study |
| **EU** | European Union |
| **Europe-HWC** | Europe-High Wood Consumption |
| **EUTR** | European Union Timber Regulation |
| **FAO** | Food and Agriculture Organization of the United Nations |
| **FORMASAM** | Forest Management Scenarios for Adaptation and Mitigation |
| **FRA** | Global Forest Resources Assessment |
| **FSC** | Forest Stewardship Council |
| **FSOS** | Forest Sector Outlook Study |
| **GDP** | gross domestic product |
| **GFPM** | Global Forest Products Model |
| **GHG** | Greenhouse Gas |
| **Gt** | Gigatonne |
| **ha** | hectare(s) |
| **HFA** | High Forest Area Scenario |
| **HWC** | High Wood Consumption |
| **HWFC** | High Wood Fibre Consumption |
| **HWP** | Harvested Wood Products |
| **IIASA** | International Institute of Applied System Analysis |
| **ILO** | International Labour Organization |
| **IPBES** | Intergovernmental Platform on Biodiversity and Ecosystem Services |
| **IPCC** | Intergovernmental Panel on Climate Change |
| **ITTO** | International Tropical Timber Organization |
| **IUCN** | International Union for Conservation of Nature |
| **Kg** | kilogram |
| **LVL** | Laminated Veneer Lumber |
| **$m^2$** | square metre(s) |
| **$m^3$** | cubic metre(s) |
| **MDF** | medium-density fibreboard |
| **MMCF** | Man-made cellulosic fibres |
| **MT** | Metric ton or tonne |
| **NA** | Not Applicable |
| **NAFSOS** | North American Forest Sector Outlook Study |
| **NPP** | Net Primary Productivity |
| **NTM** | Non-Tariff Measure |
| **NYDF** | New York Declaration on Forests |
| **OECD** | Organization for Economic Co-operation and Development |
| **PEFC** | Programme for the Endorsement of Forest Certification |
| **QR** | Quick Response code |
| **RCP** | Representative Concentration Pathways |
| **RED** | Renewable Energy Directive |
| **REU** | FAO Regional Office for Europe and Central Asia |
| **SDGs** | Sustainable Development Goals |
| **SFI** | Sustainable Forestry Initiative |
| **SFM** | Sustainable Forest Management |
| **SSP** | Shared Socioeconomic Pathways |
| **$tCO_2e$** | metric tonnes of carbon dioxide equivalent |
| **Textile-HFWC** | The Textile-High Wood Fibre Consumption |
| **UN** | United Nations |
| **UNCTAD** | United Nations Conference on Trade and Development |
| **UNDESA** | United Nations Department of Economic and Social Affairs |
| **UNECE** | United Nations Economic Commission for Europe |
| **UNEP** | United Nations Environment Programme |
| **UNFCCC** | United Nations Framework Convention on Climate Change |
| **UNFF** | United Nations Forum on Forests |
| **UNSPF** | United Nations Strategic Plan for Forests |
| **USDA** | United States Department of Agriculture |
| **USFS** | United States Forest Service |
| **WTO** | World Trade Organization |

# 1 Introduction

## Key points

- The objective of this study is to provide support for decisions affecting the long-term outlook for the forest sector of the UNECE region.

- Through scenario analysis and literature review, it offers the possibility for stakeholders to evaluate the long-term consequences of policy choices.

- The study thus intends to contribute to evidence-based policy formulation and decision making. It is not a forecast of what will happen in future. Rather, it sheds light on the possible consequences of policy choices and of factors external to the forest sector, most notably anthropogenic climate change.

- Policymakers chose two key areas of interest for the analysis: the effects of structural changes and of climate change on the UNECE forest products market and and identified six key questions important for decision-makers (see Table 1.1).

- The study takes a pragmatic, transparent and objective approach to answering these key questions, sometimes using a modeling approach – to explore consequences of choices, not to make forecasts.

- The study uses modeling results from the Global Forest Products Model (GFPM) with scenarios up to 2040.

- The study is the first to cover the whole UNECE region and provides results for all UNECE subregions - Europe, North America and Eastern Europe, Caucasus and Central Asia (EECCA).

## 1.1 Objectives

### *Why conduct an outlook study?*

We are living in a fast-changing world. However, in the midst of this uncertainty, strategic decisions must be made, whose outcomes and impacts might only become apparent several years or even decades later. This is true especially for forests and forest products, where more than a generation's lifetime can lie between planting and harvest. In addition, forests are complex ecosystems with important linkages to water, soil, and biodiversity, providing a wide range of goods and services. Thus, decisions about policies for the future of forests and their products are highly complex. They might also require difficult trade-offs between economic objectives, impacts on the labour market, environmental protection, climate change mitigation and adaptation, as well as other strategically important concerns.

The objective of this study is to provide support to these decisions. Through scenario analysis, stakeholders can evaluate the long-term consequences of their policy choices or structural changes on which they have little influence. The study thus aims to contribute to evidence-based and transparent policy formulation and decision-making.

The audience for this study includes both public and private sector decision-makers, as well as other stakeholders in the forest sector.

## 1.2 Mandate and background

### *How does this study relate to earlier studies and how was it developed?*

This Forest Sector Outlook Study is part of the Warsaw Integrated Programme of Work for the period of 2018 - 2021, which was adopted during the Joint Session of the United Nations Economic Commission for Europe (UNECE) Committee on Forests and the Forest Industry and the Food and Agriculture Organization (FAO) European Forestry Commission in Warsaw in October 2017. The publication of a sector outlook study is an output of Work Area 2, Policy Dialogue and Advice.

The series of Forest Sector Outlook Studies (FSOS) began in 1952 with the first European Timber Trend Study (ETTS I). It was followed by ETTS II to ETTS V and the first European Forest Sector Outlook Study (EFSOS), which enlarged the scope of the studies beyond forest products. The latest publications were EFSOS II (published in 2011), and the North American Forest Sector Outlook Study (NAFSOS, published in 2012), both of which covered the period 2010-2030. After their publication, several meetings reflected on the development of the studies and initiated preparation of the process for the next. As part of the consultations with the UNECE/FAO Working Party on Forest Statistics, Economics and Management in 2018, delegates agreed that this outlook study should run scenarios up to 2040, while covering in a single study the whole UNECE region with an integrated modeling framework for all subregions, i.e. Europe, North America, the Russian Federation, and Eastern Europe, Caucasus and Central Asia (EECCA).[1]

The development of this study involved many stakeholders and experts in an open and participatory process. A two-day brainstorming workshop, with representatives from the public and private sectors, together with international organizations and academia, initiated the project. They identified key trends and issues, that were translated into related key questions for decision-makers. The UNECE/FAO Forestry and Timber Section managed the work with guidance and support from the UNECE/FAO Team of Specialists on Forest Sector Outlook. Two additional UNECE/FAO Teams of Specialists provided useful feedback and input: the teams on Forest Policy and on Green Jobs. In 2018 and 2019, project updates and preliminary results were presented to the Joint UNECE/FAO Working Party on Forest Statistics, Economics and Management. During these sessions, delegates prioritized the key questions, decided on the time horizon and geographic coverage, and provided general feedback and guidance.[2]

## 1.3 Key questions for this outlook study

During the participatory process described in section 1.2, stakeholders decided on key areas for analysis in this outlook study. The two priority areas they identified were structural change in the forest sector and climate change.

Major structural changes are taking place around the world, including changes in economic growth, shifting production patterns across the globe, and developments in innovative wood-based products, such as cross-laminated timber (CLT) and man-made cellulosic fibres. The consequences of these dynamics for the UNECE forest sector deserve an in-depth analysis.

A second key concern is how climate change might affect the forest sector. The impacts of climate change are becoming more evident, and governments face increasing public pressure to react with effective policies. The sector's role as both sink and source of carbon, as well as a major carbon store (in forests and harvested wood products) make this analysis particularly complex.

Structural changes and climate change are global in nature. Consequently, a study covering the whole UNECE region with a global forest sector model – rather than putting the focus on subregions or individual countries – is well-suited as a geographic scope. Nevertheless, some impacts are more local

1 For a list of countries in the UNECE region and its subregions can be found in the Annex.

2 For detailed information on the process see ECE/TIM/WP.2/Inf3.

or regional, especially climate change effects and adaptation strategies. For these topics, regional analyses and case studies were added.

Policymakers formulated six key questions to address impacts from structural changes and climate change (Table 1.1). The whole study is structured around the answers to these six key questions.

## 1.4 Methodology

The study takes a pragmatic, transparent and objective approach to answering the key questions. In many cases, it uses a modeling approach, comparing scenarios built upon on these key questions to a reference ("business-as-usual") scenario, thereby exploring the consequences of policy choices or structural change. When a scenario approach was feasible, it was based on output from the Global Forest Products Model (GFPM), which is a dynamic economic equilibrium model of the world forest sector, describing how world forests and their industries interact through international trade (Buongiorno *et al.*, 2003). The beginning of chapter 3 provides an overview of the different scenarios and how they link to the key questions.

Models cannot capture all relevant aspects for an outlook study. Therefore, additional quantitative and qualitative information from existing research appears throughout the study, especially in the chapter on climate change.

All models and the scenarios they generate are constrained by the assumptions, methods and data used, and are, of necessity, simplifications of reality, for the purposes of analysis. For these reasons, the scenario results must be viewed with caution – they provide a rough idea of potential impacts and are not meant to be interpreted as a precise outcome, nor as a forecast.

## 1.5 Structure of the outlook study

Chapter 2 provides background information to the most important current trends and focuses on changes in demographics, economy, society, and the environment.

Chapter 3 analyses structural changes and their possible effects on UNECE forest products' markets. The first section considers the effects of changes in demand, due to different economic developments, or the acceptance of new wood products. The second discusses structural supply changes, including the effects of a potential increased wood production from outside the UNECE region, as well as the effects of natural disturbances. The third section examines trade issues and the possible effects of trade restrictions.

Chapter 4 focuses on climate change, first analyzing the impacts on UNECE forests. Second, it looks into climate change mitigation notably through the forest sink and through carbon storage in harvested wood products. It also explores the potential for mitigating climate change by substituting wood-based products for products based on less renewable materials. Third, it considers adaptation to climate change in the forest sector. Last, it discusses the challenge of balancing climate change impacts, mitigation and adaptation.

Chapter 5 briefly reviews cross-cutting issues that are important for the forest sector outlook but are not covered by the key questions and thus do not form part of the in-depth analyses in chapters 3 and 4: biodiversity, workforce, the COVID-19 pandemic and the link to the SDGs.

Chapter 6 summarizes the results and proposes food for further thought.

**TABLE 1.1 Seven thematic areas for future green forest jobs with corresponding examples**

| | Structural Changes | chapter 3 |
|---|---|---|
| **Demand for wood products** | How would different demand changes affect the UNECE forest product markets? | 3.4 |
| **Wood supply** | How would different supply changes affect the UNECE forest product markets? | 3.5 |
| **Trade** | How would significant trade restrictions affect the UNECE forest product markets? | 3.6 |
| | **Climate Change** | **chapter 4** |
| **Impacts** | How will UNECE forests be affected by climate change? | 4.2 |
| **Mitigation** | How could UNECE forests and the forest sector contribute to climate change mitigation? | 4.3 |
| **Adaptation** | How could UNECE forests adapt to climate change? | 4.4 |

# 2 Global trends

## Key points

- The UNECE region accounts for 42% of the world's forests and 47% of global forest carbon stock. It also provides 60% of global production of industrial roundwood.
- The world's population will reach 9.2 billion by 2040, and the median age will continue to increase.
- The world economy is expected to double in less than 40 years, with faster growth in emerging economies, notably in the Asia-Pacific region, and higher per capita Gross Domestic Procuct projected for all regions.
- Trade has been growing fast and is anticipated to increase further, albeit slower than in the past. Non-tariff measures, including, for the forest sector, phytosanitary regulations, log export bans or requirements for certificates of legality or sustainability, will continue to impact global trade.
- Technology will continue to drive developments in production and consumption, but it is particularly hard to project over the long term.
- Value chains have become longer and more complex, although this might change with increased automation of manufacture and rising concerns about the security of extended supply chains.
- Urbanization and a decline in household size will continue to influence the forest sector through changing consumption patterns.
- Climate change will have a major influence, which is discussed in chapter 4.
- Forests are one of the most important reservoirs of global biodiversity, whose state remains a matter of great concern, as the pressures driving the decline in biodiversity are intensifying.
- It is too early to say whether the COVID-19 pandemic will have long term consequences for the forest sector.
- Digitally enhanced data collection across the forest product value chain could boost its productivity and efficiency.
- The impact of urbanization on forests is complex, affecting the ways how forests are managed, the demand for products and services, workforce availability in rural areas, and forest ownership.

## 2.1 Introduction

Trends in economic and social development, demographics, technology, and the natural environment at the regional and global level will influence the role that forests, and their products, will play. This chapter outlines some of these global trends and their potential effects on forests and related industries, based on available literature and modelling approaches taken by different expert groups.[3]

The chapter opens with an overview of the relative importance of the UNECE region in the global forest sector (section 2.2), followed by a brief description of some major global economic, demographic, socio-economic and environmental trends (sections 2.3 to 2.6). For each "megatrend", there is a brief explanation of possible consequences for and interactions with the forest sector (in italics). Section 2.7 briefly discusses the COVID-19 pandemic in the context of global trends.

## 2.2 Relative importance of the UNECE region's forests, forest products and carbon stock

This brief section puts the forests of the UNECE region in their global context.

In 2020, the UNECE region was home to 42% of the world's forests and 49% of the world's primary forest (FAO, 2020a). Furthermore, 85% of the global certified forest area is located in UNECE member States (UNECE/FAO, 2017).

The global forest area continued to decline in the period 2010 to 2015 with annual losses estimated at 4.7 million ha, moderately less than the 5.2 million ha lost annually from 2000 to 2010. Strong regional differences exist. The bulk of the decline has taken place in Africa, Central and South America, and Southern and South East Asia, where the main type of forest that has been lost was tropical forest. In terms of forests by climatic zone, deforestation has been lowest in boreal and temperate forests. In contrast to these global declining trends, in all parts of the UNECE region forest area has been expanding (FAO, 2020a).

The UNECE region has been, and continues to be, a major player in global forest products' market. In 2018, the region accounted for 60% of global industrial roundwood production, 63% of sawnwood production, and 53% of fibre furnish (wood pulp and recovered paper) (FAOSTAT, 2021). However, over the long term this share has been diminishing as other regions experience increase in demand and develop their own forest sector and wood processing industries. Around 1960, the UNECE region accounted for more than 80% of global manufacturing of forest products. By 2018, this share had fallen down to 60% for industrial roundwood, 45% for paper and paperboard, and below 40% for wood-based panels (FAOSTAT 2021).

The forest carbon stock, including soil carbon, in the UNECE region, rose from 293 Gt in 1990 to 311 Gt in 2020, an increase of 6%. Globally over this period, there was a slight decrease in total forest carbon stock. Thus, over the 30-year period, the UNECE region's share of global forest carbon stock has risen from 44% to 47% (FAO, 2020a).

## 2.3 Economic trends

**Gross Domestic Product (GDP) growth and the importance of emerging markets:** Projecting economic growth beyond a few years is challenging, given the level of uncertainty and the unpredictability of future events. Nevertheless, long-term projections, like the one prepared by PwC and presented below, can still deliver interesting insights into main trends and patterns.

Assuming continued technology-driven productivity improvements, global GDP is projected to grow by 130% between 2016 and 2050. Thus, the world economy would more than double in less than 40 years, far surpassing projected population growth. On this basis, world per capita income is projected to rise for the next three decades. Growth estimates differ between countries and regions and the results imply major shifts in the global economy. The emerging markets of Brazil, China, India, Indonesia, Mexico, the Russian Federation, and Turkey, are projected to expand their share of global GDP and to grow, on average, around twice as fast as the advanced economies of Canada, France, Germany, Italy, Japan, the United Kingdom, and the United States of America. However per capita income, by 2050, is projected to remain higher in Europe and North America than in the emerging economies (PwC, 2017).

**Trade:** After 1945, increasing globalization of production and consumption triggered rapid growth of international trade. In 1950, roughly 8% of total global production was exported, a figure that grew up to 24% by 2014 (Ortiz-Ospina *et al.*, 2018).

Though overall trade in goods continues to increase in absolute terms, today the rate of growth in trade and overall trade intensity (the ratio of gross exports to gross output) are decreasing in nearly all goods-producing value chains. To a large extent this has been a result of growing domestic demand in China and other emerging economies. In these countries, more comprehensive domestic supply chains led to a lower dependence on imports and a higher consumption of domestic production (Lund *et al.*, 2019).

Non-tariff measures (NTMs), such as sanitary and phytosanitary measures, technical barriers to trade, or price-control measures for imported goods, also impact global trade. Common examples are phytosanitary regulations to limit the risk of spreading diseases, or the requirement to provide certificates of sustainability or assurances of legality under the European

3 The trends highlighted in this chapter provide a general background and are not related to the modelling procedure based on Shared Socioeconomic Pathways (SSPs) presented in chapter 3.

Union (EU) Timber Regulation (EUTR[4]) in the EU or the Lacey Act[5] in the US, and log export bans designed to limit or prevent exports of raw materials (UNECE/FAO, 2017). A study by the United Nations Conference on Trade and Development and the World Bank concluded that NTMs have a bigger influence on global trade than tariffs. This especially applies to agricultural products, machinery and other manufactured goods, as well as wood products (UNCTAD and Worldbank, 2018).

The role of trade in the global forest sector is fully integrated into the Global Forest Products Model which is the basis for most of the scenarios in chapter 3. This aspect is therefore not discussed here any further.

Value chains have also become more complex in the forest sector, and both raw materials and products are being traded internationally over long distances. However, this might change as automation is strengthening the efficiency and precision of production processes thereby limiting the importance of lower labour costs for manufacturing. In such context proximity to markets may become a more significant factor than labour expenditures when companies take decisions about where to locate (Lund *et al.*, 2019).

**Technology:** Technological development in many sectors is perhaps the dominant driving force in the global economy today: It is influencing, indeed creating, markets, generating new products and manufacturing methods and improving the competitive advantage of companies, sector and countries. It is however very difficult, if not impossible to make long term robust scenarios for technological development.

Technological innovation will affect the forest sector in many ways: satellite and drone technologies are already transforming forest inventory, blockchain and other secure communication techniques can strengthen chain-of-custody processes, e-commerce plays a major role in determining the needs for packaging materials (Näyhä *et al.*, 2014). Information technology has reduced production and transport costs, biorefineries are developing new wood-based products, genetic engineering has the potential to increase increment of plantation trees. All these factors make forecasting future demand in wood-based products particularly complex and uncertain.

Despite the importance of technology for the forest sector, no attempt has been made to construct scenarios based on the technology factor because of the extreme difficulty of creating robust and transparent assumptions about long term trends in technological development.

4 https://ec.europa.eu/environment/forests/timber_regulation.htm.

5 https://www.fws.gov/international/laws-treaties-agreements/us-conservation-laws/lacey-act.html.

## 2.4 Demographic trends

**Population growth:** The United Nations (UN) projects for the world population to rise from 7.7 billion in 2019 to almost 9.2 billion by 2040 and 9.7 billion by 2050 (Figure 2.1). That said, population increase will vary significantly between regions, with the biggest growth happening in Africa and Asia, and relative stagnation in most parts of the UNECE region.

FIGURE 2.1 CURRENT AND PROJECTED GLOBAL POPULATION

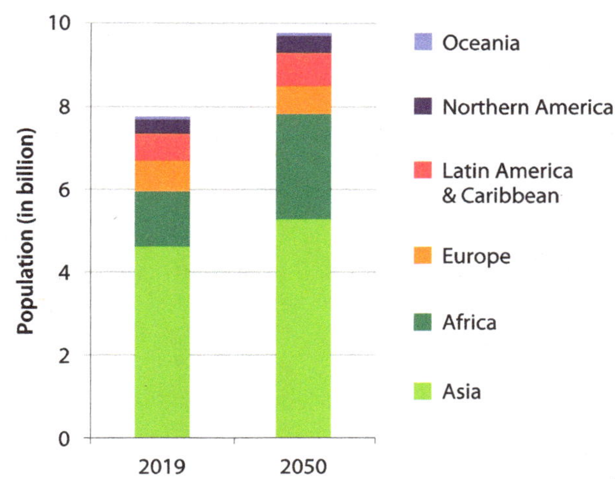


**Note:** Regions defined according to UNDESA, 2019a.
**Source:** UNDESA, 2019a.

Population size, with GDP, are the main determinants of total demand for forest products. Population projections are fully integrated into the scenarios presented in chapter 3.

**Ageing:** The world's population is predicted to continue its ageing trend between 2020 and 2050. In 2000, the global median age was 26.3 years. By 2015, it had risen to 29.6 years, and is predicted to reach 36.2 years by 2050. By 2050 over-60s are forecast to make up 21% of the world's population and will be more numerous than children below the age of 15 years (UNDESA, 2019a). The population of most UNECE countries is older than the global average.

The housing market is the major demand driver for solid wood products (sawnwood and panels), whether in construction or in furniture. As population ages, and household formation changes there is likely to be an impact on housing markets, both quantitative and qualitative (type of housing).

## 2.5 Socio-economic trends

**Urbanization:** Urban population has been increasing its share of the total for many years. In 2018, 55% of the global population were living in urban areas. Recent projections indicate that this proportion will grow to 60% in 2030, and 68% by 2050.

Urbanization will not rise equally across regions: Europe as well as Latin and North America already have high levels of urbanization, up to 80%, compared to 40% in Africa and 50% in Asia, where most global urban growth is expected by 2050 (UNDESA, 2019b).

Urbanization puts pressure on land use in urban areas thus influencing the type of construction (probably more intense and multi-storey than in rural areas). The phenomenon also changes rural ownership patterns (e.g. by pushing up the number of absentees – urban – forest owners), modifies demand for forest services, notably recreation in peri-urban areas, reduces rural labour supply and changes public perceptions of forests and how they should be managed.

**Household size:** Demand for housing is not only driven by the numbers and types of households as well as the overall population but also the average number of members living together in one household. Household composition is expected to shift since the average number of people in each household will decline. For instance, in the United States, the average number of people per household decreased from 2.8 in 1980 to 2.5 in 2020 (U.S. Census Bureau, 2019). This reduction in household size means that the number of households generally grows faster than the population size (Bradbury, Peterson and Liu, 2014). Causes for this trend are the decline in household size - include elderly people living alone, higher levels of divorce, and career-oriented young people living by themselves. The fall in household size may lead to an increase in housing demand in some regions.

## 2.6 Environmental changes

**Climate change:** The 2018 report of the Intergovernmental Panel on Climate Change (IPCC) concluded that anthropogenic climate change has reached around 1°C above pre-industrial levels and is likely to exceed 1.5°C warming within the next 10-30 years unless there are dramatic reductions in carbon emissions (IPCC, 2018).

The emissions of 57 countries (representing 60% of global emissions) have peaked already or the countries have a commitment that implies a peak by 2030. However, this is not enough to meet the objectives under the Paris Agreement, which stipulates holding long-term temperature increases well below 2°C and to work to limit the increase to 1.5°C.

The consequences of climate change for UNECE forests, and their possible contribution to climate change mitigation and adaptation are analysed in depth in chapter 4.

**Biodiversity:** The state of biodiversity and species abundance worldwide continues to deteriorate, driven by direct factors such as land and sea use changes, overexploitation of natural resources, pollution, and the effects of invasive species on natural ecosystems. According to the Secretariat of the Convention of Biological Diversity (2020), the current rate of decline is unprecedented, while the pressures driving this decline are intensifying. Estimates suggest that around 25% of species in assessed animal and plant groups are currently threatened by extinction and roughly 9% of the world's terrestrial species are living in a habitat insufficient for long-term survival, mostly as a result of human action. Global indicators of ecosystem extent and condition have shown a decrease by an average of 47% of their estimated natural baselines and most terrestrial biomes have shown a decline of 20% in native species abundance. (IPBES, 2019)

Forests are one of the most important reservoirs of global biodiversity. They contain 60,000 tree species, 80% of amphibian species, 75% of bird species, and 68% of the world's mammal species. Their sustainable management is therefore essential for biodiversity conservation. Eighteen percent of the world's forests are in legally protected areas (FAO, 2018; FAO, 2019; FAO, 2020a and b). Biodiversity conservation is an essential part of sustainable forest management, and as such coexists and interacts with the other components. Thus, structural changes in forest product markets and the impact of climate change will strongly influence the ability of the UNECE region's forests to conserve biodiversity.

It was not possible with the methods and resources available to analyse these interactions in the present study[6] although they are briefly reviewed in section 5.2.

## 2.7 Impact of the COVID-19 pandemic on global trends for the forest sector

The COVID-19 pandemic has had major negative effects on global health, but also on the economy, with a major recession in 2020 and 2021. In mid-2021, some countries and sectors are starting to recover from the health and economic crises, while some sectors have been less affected or have actually been stimulated by the radical changes cause by the pandemic. At present, it is not possible to say how this will impact longer term projections, like those in this study.

It is too soon to analyse the long-term impacts, if any, of COVID-19 on the forest sector. The issue is briefly reviewed in section 5.5.

6 The policy questions linked to conserving biodiversity were analysed in EFSOS II, for Europe only.

# 3 Structural changes in the forest sector and forest product markets

## Key points

- The reference scenario projects an increase in forest area and wood production in the UNECE region. Consumption and production of forest products is also expected to grow, and prices rise slightly.

- Structural increases in demand outside the UNECE region, for instance due to higher use of wood by the Chinese housing sector, would increase roundwood production and prices also inside and outside the UNECE region, and increase the region's net exports.

- Structural increases in demand inside the UNECE region, for instance due to an increased share of wood in construction, would also increase roundwood production and cause higher roundwood prices. European net exports would be lower than in the reference scenario, while Russian roundwood exports would be higher.

- If wood-based fibres increased their share of the textile market to 30%, global roundwood production would be 81 million $m^3$ higher than in the reference scenario, mostly from the UNECE region, and roundwood prices would rise, negatively affecting production of sawnwood and panels.

- In all three higher demand scenarios, forest growing stock in the UNECE region continued to increase, although more slowly than in the reference scenario.

- If global forest area expanded by 10%, in accordance with policy objectives, roundwood production would be 2% higher, and prices for roundwood, sawnwood and panels would be lower than in the reference scenario.

- If there were a rapid increase in planted forest, mostly outside the UNECE region, prices would fall, and consumption and production of forest products would increase.

- At present, the consequences of natural disturbances in forests (wildfire, insects, pathogens, storms, drought) are mostly limited in time and space, and absorbed by market adjustments, notably salvage felling. However, the long-term future impacts of disturbances on global markets due to climate change are unknown, and further research is needed.

- Published research indicates clearly that higher tariffs, and non-tariff barriers to trade in forest products, depress overall economic output in the forest sector, although in each circumstance, there are winners and losers.

## 3.1 Introduction

This chapter addresses the key questions about the possible consequences for the forest sector of structural changes in demand, supply or trade of forest products. This chapter is based on a full academic study which is being published separately as "Structural changes in the forest sector and their long term consequences for the forest sector: a contribution to the Forest Sector Outlook Study 2020-2040" in the series of UNECE/FAO Discussion Papers. This chapter summarises the full analysis. Readers who need more information on the sources, methods and results should consult the full study.

This chapter summarises the full analysis and focuses more on the results than on the methodology. Readers who need more information on the sources, methods and results should consult the full study.

This chapter briefly presents the analytical concepts used, and the reference scenario – what is projected if there are no structural changes in the forest sector. Then it presents the possible consequences of seven structural changes, each addressing one of the key questions identified for the study.

## 3.2 Methodology

The main analytical tool has been the elaboration of a number of 'what-if' scenarios using the Global Forest Products Model (GFPM) (Buongiorno *et al.*, 2003, Buongiorno and Zhu, 2018).

Through the model, changes in per capita income, rural population density, and labour force per unit of forest area result in projections of forest area (total and planted) by country, which in turn drive trends in forest growing stock. The availability of roundwood to meet the demands of industry in countries will reflect the area, volume, and growth rates of forests. The demand for forest products at all price levels, mirrors rises and falls in disposable incomes. Market-clearing[7] conditions produce, for each period, country and product, results for final market prices, production, consumption, imports, and exports. Market-clearing conditions also provide results for net carbon sequestration and storage in standing forests and wood products. The analysis generated by the GFPM of carbon stocks and flows is in chapter 4.

This chapter focuses on how departures from recent patterns of supply and demand – i.e. structural changes – might affect the forest sector of the UNECE region. The models compare the outcomes to a reference scenario.

Not all the suggested uncertainties could be analysed with the model applied in this Outlook study. Fortunately, others have already researched some of these aspects, providing insights that are shared in this chapter.

The results are reported for five subregions: North America; Europe-EU; Europe-Other; the Russian Federation; and Eastern Europe, Caucasus and Central Asia (EECCA) (see Figure 3.1).

The scenarios cover the years 2020-2040, with 2017 as the base year for projections.

Concern has been expressed about the possible influence of the COVID-19 pandemic on the results of the long-term outlook. However, the scenarios in the Outlook study are not affected because its basic design does not address the consequences of the pandemic, and the modelling was completed before the pandemic. Despite the evident short-term consequences of the pandemic, there is at present no empirical evidence of the interactions between the pandemic and the forest sector which might modify the long-term outlook.

## 3.3 Reference scenario

### 3.3.1 *Assumptions underlying the reference scenario*

The reference scenario is based on the assumption that past trends and relationships are unaffected by structural change. It assumes that market structures, historical rates of technology change, and the climate regime remain unchanged from those observed to 2017. Projections for 2020 to 2040 follow Shared Socioeconomic Pathways (SSP) as defined by the International Institute for Applied Systems Analysis (IIASA). The SSPs are defined by the degree of challenge that societies face to either adapt to or mitigate climate change.

For this study, although three of the five SSPs were modelled for the forest sector with the GFPM - SSP2, SSP3 and SSP5- it was decided to use the scenario based on SSP2 as the reference scenario to which the what-if scenarios of structural change are compared. Projections based on SSP3 and SSP5 are presented in the full study.

The reference scenario is the "business-as-usual", "middle-of-the-road" vision of the future, where development pathways are assumed to be consistent with historical social, economic, and technological trends.

The following subsections describe the reference scenario generated by the GFPM on the basis of the SSP2 assumptions.

### 3.3.2 *Total forest area in the reference scenario*

The model assumes that per capita income change is what drives forest area. In Europe-EU, Europe-Other, the Russian Federation, and EECCA, rising per capita income is expected to result in an expansion of forest in most countries, between 2020 and 2040. Projections for North America also suggest that forest area will expand, but at a declining rate (Figure 3.1).

7 Market clearing is the process by which the supply of whatever is traded is equated to the demand through the price mechanism, so that there is no leftover supply or demand and an equilibrium price is identified.

**FIGURE 3.1** HISTORIC AND PROJECTED ANNUAL AVERAGE CHANGE IN FOREST AREA IN FIVE UNECE SUBREGIONS BY 2040

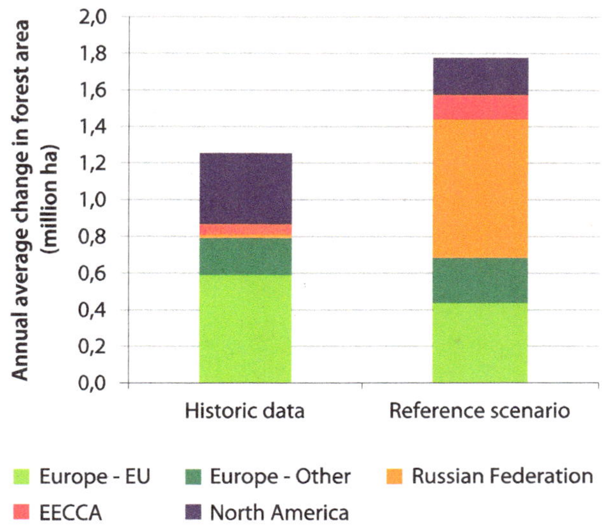


**Notes:** Historic data 1990-2015; Reference scenario 2020-2040. 2017 is the base year for projections and is the average of 2016-2018. The values for 2016-2018 have been interpolated from the 2015 forest area growth rate reported by FAO (2015b).

**Sources:** FAO, 2015b and GFPM projection.

**FIGURE 3.2** HISTORIC AND PROJECTED ANNUAL AVERAGE CHANGE IN FOREST AREA IN THE UNECE REGION AND THE REST OF THE WORLD BY 2040

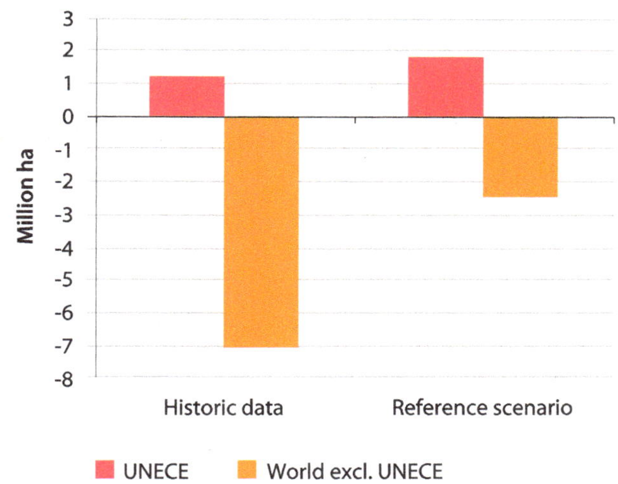


**Notes:** Historic data 1990-2015; Reference scenario 2020-2040. 2017 is the base year for projections and is the average of 2016-2018. The values for 2016-2018 have been interpolated from the 2015 forest area growth rate reported by FAO (2015b).

**Sources:** FAO, 2015b and GFPM projection.

Historically, the forest area of the Russian Federation has largely remained constant. It is the largest in the world, and mostly situated far from human settlements. In the reference scenario, the forest area in the Russian Federation is projected to expand slightly faster than in other regions, increasing by roughly 0.1% per year, between 2020 and 2040. This is due to predicted increases in per capita income, and Russia's status as a middle-income economy. The environmental Kuznets curve[8], used by the model, suggests that as incomes rise, countries experience high rates of forest expansion. The forest area expansion for the Russian Federation appears to be overestimated by GFPM, but the effect on the results are thought to be neglible as it is very small compared to the large area of forest in the Russian Federation.

Forest area for the rest of the world is projected under the reference scenario to fall, by 0.1% annually, between 2020 and 2040, a rate of change slower than in the past but in accordance with the most recently reported trends of the Global Forest Resources Assessment published by the FAO (FAO, 2020). Figure 3.2 compares the trends in forest area in the UNECE region to those in the rest of the world.

8 The environmental Kuznets curve suggests that economic development initially leads to a deterioration in the environment, but after a certain level of economic growth, a society begins to improve its relationship with the environment and, as a result, levels of environmental degradation reduce.

### 3.3.3 *Area of planted forest in the reference scenario*

The model of planted forest area change assumes that change is driven by a combination of per capita income, rural population density, and labour force per unit of forest. Projections range from slow increases to slight decreases in planted forest area in the UNECE region. In the reference scenario, Europe-Other at +14%, and North America at +12% would experience the biggest expansion between 2015 and 2040. Outside the UNECE region, the rest of the world is projected to see planted forest area expand by +14%. Forest growing stock is projected to rise steadily from 2020 to 2040 in all UNECE subregions, continuing historic patterns. However growing stock in the rest of the world is projected to continue its downward trend (Figure 3.4 and Figure 3.5). Growing stock volume is projected to increase in the UNECE region, supporting an expansion of wood processing capacity. This expansion would affect production, consumption, trade, and prices for all forest products. Between 2020 and 2040, the EECCA is projected to see the largest increase in growing stock (+47%). Projected growing stock increases for the other subregions are Europe-Other (+43%), Europe-EU (+29%), the Russian Federation (+13%), and North America (+2%).

### 3.3.4 *Forest product prices in the reference scenario*

Prices for primary and secondary wood products are projected to increase slightly in real terms, in line with increasing GDP and GDP per capita, despite increasing global forest growing stock Figure 3.3, Figure 3.4 and Figure 3.5.

The projected rise in real (inflation-adjusted) prices to 2040 is modest, and within historical price ranges variation since 1990. Such modest rises indicate no major wood scarcity.

**FIGURE 3.3** HISTORICAL AND PROJECTED ANNUAL AVERAGE CHANGE IN FOREST GROWING STOCK IN FIVE UNECE SUBREGIONS BY 2040

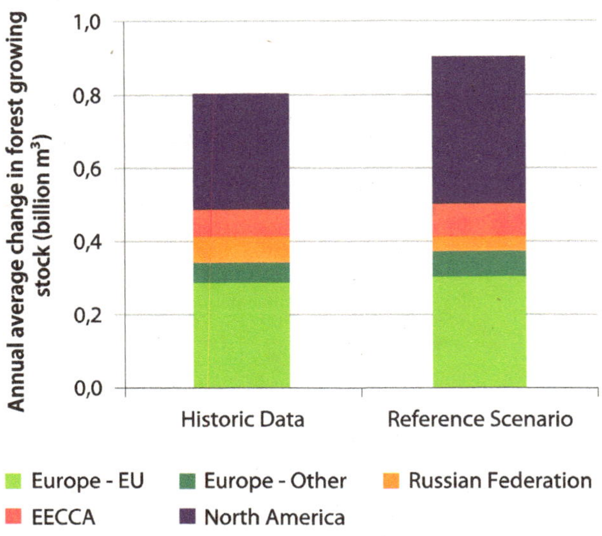


**Notes:** Historic data 1990-2015; Reference scenario 2020-2040. 2017 is the base year for projections and is the average of 2016-2018. The values for 2016-2018 have been interpolated from the 2015 forest area growth rate reported by FAO (2015b).

**Sources:** FAO, 2015b and GFPM projection.

**FIGURE 3.4** HISTORICAL AND PROJECTED ANNUAL AVERAGE CHANGE IN FOREST GROWING STOCK IN THE UNECE REGION AND THE REST OF THE WORLD

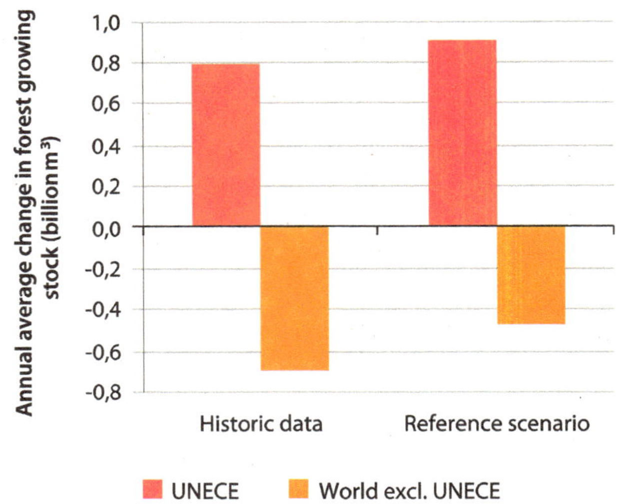


**Notes:** Historic data 1990-2015; Reference scenario 2020-2040. 2017 is the base year for projections and is the average of 2016-2018. The values for 2016-2018 have been interpolated from the 2015 forest area growth rate reported by FAO (2015b).

**Sources:** FAO, 2015b and GFPM projection.

**FIGURE 3.5** HISTORICAL AND PROJECTED WORLD PRICES FOR DIFFERENT WOOD PRODUCTS

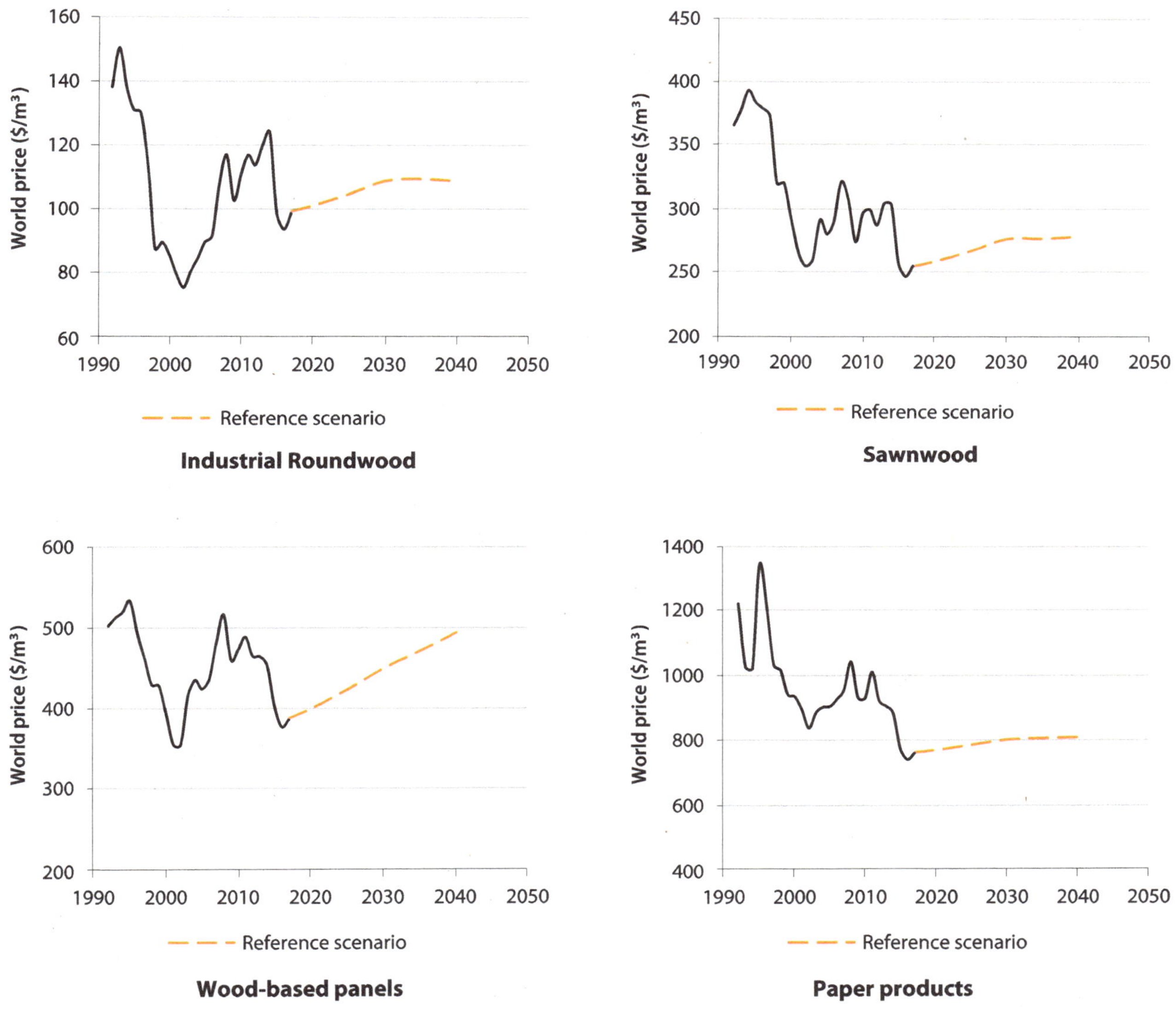


**Notes:** Historical levels 1990-2016; Reference scenario 2020-2040. 2017 is the base year for projections and is the average of 2016-2018 (FAO 2019).
Wood-based panels use the average of prices for plywood, particle board and fiberboard.
Paper products use the average of prices for newsprint, printing and writing paper, and other paper and paper board.
All prices adjusted for inflation
**Sources:** FAO, 2015b and GFPM projection.

### 3.3.5 Production, consumption and trade of forest products in the reference scenario

The reference scenario projects an increase in industrial roundwood production globally, and in every UNECE subregion. Net exports of roundwood follow historical trends: Europe-EU is projected to remain a net importer, while other UNECE subregions are projected to remain net exporters of industrial roundwood, although the net exports of the Russian Federation are projected to fall.

**Sawnwood** production is projected to rise strongly in Europe-EU, outperforming other UNECE subregions and the rest of the world. Europe-EU is projected to be an increasingly important global source of sawnwood over two decades from 2020 to 2040 and net exports of sawnwood from this subregion are projected to rise from below 20 million $m^3$ per year to more than 70 million $m^3$ per year over this period, in line with historical trends. By contrast, North America's share of total UNECE and world output is projected to fall. The Russian Federation is projected to continue as a net exporter of sawnwood. North America too is projected to remain a net exporter, but with declining volumes after 2030. Europe-Other, the EECCA, and the world excluding the UNECE region are projected to continue to be net importers of sawnwood.

Wood-based panels production is projected to rise in almost every subregion, except for North America, where overall production is projected to remain largely unchanged. The trend for panel production in North America is expected to be heterogenous, with falling particle board production which is projected to be offset by rising plywood, veneer, and fibreboard production, until 2040. Continuing recent trends, North America is projected to further increase its net imports of panels. The Russian Federation is projected to increase net exports steadily to 2040.

Pulp and paper production are projected to increase in the UNECE region through 2040. Newsprint, printing and writing paper (graphics paper) show continuing stagnation in production and consumption due primarily to electronic media substitution, while the category 'other paper and paperboard' continue to show modest growth driven by an increasing demand for tissue and packaging papers. Production of total paper and paperboard is projected to rise by about 20% in Europe-EU and to be about stable in North America. The UNECE region's share of global paper production is projected to continue to fall, although the dominant pulp and paper producers (Canada, Finland, Sweden, United States) are projected to continue as positive net exporters through to 2040. North America is projected to be an increasingly important global exporter of wood pulp, especially to China, as an input to Chinese paper manufacture.

Results for consumption of forest products generally followed projected trends in production despite projected increases in product prices. Consumption of industrial roundwood is projected to increase for most of Europe, resulting in a projected decline in net exports of roundwood. North America's consumption of sawnwood, wood-based panels, and paper products are all projected to increase more than production. As a result, North America's net exports of sawnwood are projected to fall, and its net imports of panels to rise. The subregion is projected to become a net importer of paper, instead of a net exporter. However, in that subregion, industrial roundwood production growth is projected to outstrip consumption growth, allowing an increase in net exports.

## 3.4 Scenarios for structural changes in demand

**KEY QUESTION:**

***How would different demand changes affect the UNECE forest products market?***

This section describes three 'what-if' scenarios for structural changes in demand and compares them to the reference scenario. It examines the consequences for the forest sector worldwide of three possible structural increases in demand: outside the UNECE region, inside the UNECE region and from new products, such as textiles.

In all three demand-side 'what-if' scenarios, forest area is assumed to be unaffected, and the consequences of increased wood demand are limited to its influence on forest density, (the growing stock volume per unit area of forest), which would change according to projected roundwood removals and forest stock growth. In the model, higher wood demand will increase harvesting, lowering overall average forest growing stock globally, in comparison with the reference scenario. In GFPM, a lower growing stock density leads to a relatively higher rate of forest biomass growth, an inverse relationship widely agreed in the forest science literature. The GFPM does not impose constraints on any country's timber harvests. In the model, harvests are constrained by economic variables, not by laws, national specifications of maximum (or minimum) annual allowable cuts or any assumed conception of the meaning of "sustainability".

### 3.4.1 Increased demand for wood products in China

***What if...***
***China built every tenth new housing unit with wood?***

**Scenario assumption**
**China would build every tenth new housing unit with the same volume of wood used to construct a single unit of a multifamily dwelling in the United States, in 2015.**

The China-High Wood Consumption (China-HWC) scenario models the effects on global markets of greater use of wood for construction from outside the UNECE region, using China's housing market as a proxy for stronger demand over a wider area, because of the size and significance of the Chinese market: if wood construction played a significantly greater role in China in the future, it could well influence other regions and lead to further growth in forest products markets.

Residential construction using wood as the primary building material comprises less than 0.1% of the roughly 10 million units built annually in China (Geng *et al.*, 2019). If a sudden policy change required that 10% of new housing units in China match the floor area and wood content of a typical multifamily (apartment) dwelling in the United States, the policy would induce a significant surge in worldwide demand for construction wood.

The additional demand caused by such a policy shift would require global **industrial roundwood** production (and consumption) to rise by over 270 million $m^3$ (12%), with one-third being met from domestic production in China. The higher prices for roundwood that could be expected to result from growing Chinese demand for sawnwood and panels might spur increased roundwood production of 126 million $m^3$ in the UNECE region, meeting almost half of the increased global need for roundwood.

By 2040, **sawnwood** consumption in China is projected to be almost 60% higher in this scenario compared to the reference scenario. Sawnwood production in China would probably not keep pace with this higher consumption. Capacity is projected to expand only slightly. The consumption shortfall would therefore have to be made up by importing more sawnwood, and most of that, more than 75%, is projected to come from the UNECE region.

In contrast to the results in the sawnwood sector, China is projected to meet most of its increased **wood-based panel** quantities needed to build the housing units through domestic production. The reason is that China already has an established panel manufacturing sector, which is more price-responsive. Only North America and Europe-EU are expected to export significantly more panels to China. Production and consumption of **paper** in the UNECE region and globally are not expected to be significantly affected in this scenario.

The extra demand for wood in China is projected to lead to world roundwood **prices** by 2040 which are 9% higher than in the reference scenario. Sawnwood and panel prices are also projected to be higher than in the reference scenario, by 8% and 3% respectively.

**Forest growing stock** in the UNECE region would be less than 1% lower than in the reference scenario. In China, however, the sharp increase in domestic roundwood production is projected to lead to forest growing stock 7% lower than in the reference scenario. Despite these lower values compared to the reference scenario, forest growing stock would still increase in absolute terms.

Table 3.1 provides an overview on the main outcomes of the scenario.

### 3.4.2 *Increased wood construction in Europe and the Russian Federation*

***What if...***

***Europe and the Russian Federation significantly increased the amount of wood used in construction?***

**Scenario assumption**

**Per capita consumption of sawnwood and wood-based structural panels in Europe and the Russian Federation would rise steadily from 2020 to 2040, to match 2015 levels in the United States.**

The Europe-High Wood Consumption (Europe-HWC) scenario simulates how increased wood consumption within the UNECE region would affect markets. Factors that might result in higher wood consumption in Europe and the Russian Federation include:

- Changes in international building standards, allowing larger and taller wood-frame structures (American Wood Council, 2018).
- Increased availability and acceptance of mass timber[9] products, including cross-laminated timber (CLT) and glulam beams, by architects, builders, and property owners (The Beck Group, 2018, Breneman *et al.*, 2019).
- Policies and programmes encouraging the use of wood in construction, as part of climate change mitigation measures.
- Higher prices of non-wood substitutes.

All these factors have been intensively discussed and some are actively promoted at the policy level. Forecasts indicate that the market for mass timber will grow significantly. Indeed, its consumption has been rising fast in recent years.

In this scenario, **industrial roundwood** production in the UNECE region would be 54 million $m^3$, or 4%, higher in 2040 than in the reference scenario. Globally, roundwood prices would be 4% higher and production would increase by 90 million $m^3$ by 2040 as countries beyond the UNECE region would help to meet the global demand in Europe and the Russian Federation. Consumption of roundwood also increased in line with the assumed increase in sawnwood and panel demand in the UNECE region. The exception was the Russian Federation, where consumption of industrial roundwood

9 Mass timber is understood as multiple solid wood panels nailed or glued together, which provide exceptional strength and stability.

fell, as producers took advantage of higher global prices to increase net exports, an outcome enabled by the widening gap between low domestic prices and higher export prices.

Production of **sawnwood** increased in Europe to meet the stronger demand, while net exports from this subregion were less than in the reference scenario. Sawnwood production was higher than in the reference scenario by 16% in Europe-EU and Europe-Other and 26% in EECCA, with smaller differences in North America and globally. The higher consumption modelled in Europe and the Russian Federation under this scenario results in additional 66 million $m^3$ of sawnwood consumed within the UNECE region, with most of that in Europe-EU. An interesting outcome of generally higher sawnwood prices is that sawnwood production in the Russian Federation is projected to fall, while net exports would decline by 16 million $m^3$ as the Russian Federation exports roundwood to be made into sawnwood in the EU. In total, net exports of sawnwood from the UNECE region are 34% lower than in the reference scenario, with only North America increasing net exports compared to the reference scenario.

The difference in **wood-based panel** consumption for Europe and the Russian Federation compared to the reference scenario is smaller than that for sawnwood. Production of wood-based panels is 8% higher in the UNECE region. Effects on the **paper sector** were insignificant.

In line with expectations, world prices would be higher for all products, not only for roundwood. Higher product prices outside Europe and the Russian Federation, would lead to lower consumption and higher net exports from these regions to partially satisfy the higher demand in Europe and the Russian Federation.

Higher prices and higher rates of harvesting in the UNECE region are projected to result in 1% smaller **forest growing stock** than in the reference scenario by 2040. The effect on growing stock in the UNECE region is projected to be much smaller than the effect on growing stock in China in the China-HWC scenario. Though Europe would be more reliant on imports of industrial roundwood from outside the region, the effect on global forest growing stock would also be minimal. In absolute terms, forest growing stock in the UNECE region, and globally, is projected to grow between 2020 and 2040 in both the 'what-if' and the reference scenarios.

Table 3.2 provides an overview on the main outcomes of the scenario.

### 3.4.3 *Increased demand for wood-based textiles*

***What if...***
***the textile sector replaced 30% of its fibre intake with wood-based fibres?***

**Scenario assumption**
**Global demand for textile fibre will continue to grow steadily from 2020 to 2040. Wood-based fibres would partially replace polyester and cotton, to make up 30% of the total fibre demand of the textile sector by 2040.**

Global fibre demand almost doubled between 2000 and 2019. With similar growth rates in the future, global textile fibre demand could reach 222 million tonnes by 2040. Currently, synthetic fibres made from oil (mainly polyester) dominate the market. Man-made cellulosic fibres (MMCFs) account for 6% (Textile Exchange, 2020).

There is an argument that modern wood-based fibres have a superior environmental footprint over other main fibre types (Hurmekoski et al, 2018). Modern wood-based fibres, such as Lyocell, are already in commercial production, and constitute 4.3% of the MMCF market share.

The Textile-High Wood Fibre Consumption (Textile-HWFC) scenario examines the consequences for the sector of a possible significant increase in the use of wood as feedstock for textiles, replacing oil-based fibres.

The demand for sustainable wood-based fibres is forecast by some analysts to maintain rapid growth as manufacturers look increasingly to become more sustainable. Given this positive outlook, wood-based fibres may partially compensate for declining demand in the graphic paper sector (Hurmekoski *et al.*, 2018).

The modelling of this scenario assumed that 53 million additional tonnes of wood based fibres, the equivalent of 265 additional $m^3$ of roundwood, would be supplied by the top ten wood pulp producing countries, based on their current shares of global wood pulp production (FAO 2019).

In this scenario, global **roundwood prices** are projected to be slightly higher by 2040 than in the reference scenario. Higher roundwood prices would make sawnwood and panel manufacture more expensive, which would reduce their production as well as their consumption. Likewise, higher roundwood prices would lead to a in the production of wood pulp for the paper sector and consequently higher paper prices and lower paper production. Those effects are not explicitly quantified in this study.

The increased demand from the textile sector, over and above the reference scenario, was projected to boost **industrial roundwood** supply globally by 81 million $m^3$, of which 51 million $m^3$ would arise in the UNECE region. The consumption of industrial roundwood likewise increased in the UNECE region, but the magnitude of the projected increase in consumption was higher than the projected increases in production, leading to lower net exports. An exception to this trend was observed for the Russian Federation, where consumption of roundwood was 12 million $m^3$ lower than in the reference scenario by 2040. This effect is largely due to significantly lower projected domestic prices compared to global roundwood prices, making it more profitable to export roundwood than to consume it domestically.

More costly industrial roundwood inputs to the **sawnwood and panels** sectors in the UNECE region due to the stronger demand for raw material for textiles lead to a reduction in production of both sawnwood and panels. Production of sawnwood is 26 million $m^3$ less than in the reference scenario, Globally the effects are smaller, as some of the reduced production in the UNECE region is offset by higher production in non-UNECE countries, such as China, with smaller relative changes in their sawnwood manufacturing costs. Consequently, sawnwood exports from the UNECE region decrease, while China reduces its net imports. The higher cost of industrial roundwood inputs to the panels sector has effects that are substantially smaller than those in the sawnwood sector, due to wood's relatively smaller share of total manufacturing cost in panel production.

Finally, this scenario results in slightly **smaller forest growing stock** compared to the reference scenario, both in the UNECE region and globally by 2040. The small changes emerge because of the offsetting effects of reduced wood products (sawnwood, panels) production and increased wood fibre production to meet the new demands of the textiles sector. Nevertheless, UNECE regional and total global stocks rise steadily through 2040 in this scenario, continuing recent trends.

Note that the GPFM does not directly model the "cascading" uses of wood, so there are no directly estimated parameters that quantify the volumes, value, or transfers of sawmill residues. The results of the textiles scenario depend on how the GPFM accounts for the higher value of sawmilling co-products on the sawmill and wood panel industries. The projected changes therefore need to be viewed with a degree of caution.

There is one more caveat. The scenario applies an across-the-board increase in pulp demand to the ten countries that are the largest producers of dissolving pulp. It is unlikely that the increased production of fibre would be delivered in such an evenly spread manner. Nevertheless, the overall direction of change in these variables is indicative of the impacts that could be expected.

Table 3.3 provides an overview on the main outcomes of the scenario.

## 3.5 Structural supply changes

**KEY QUESTION:**

***How would different supply changes affect the UNECE forest product market?***

Increases in global forest growing stock, making more timber available for harvest, could occur through policies or programmes to foster forest expansion or increase growing stock volume per hectare. This section explores the possible consequences for the sector of changes in supply, whether resulting from increased forest area, or increased plantation area.

### *3.5.1 Increased global forest area*

***What if...***
***the global forest area was 10% greater?***

**Scenario assumption**
**By 2040, the global forest area would be 4.4 billion ha or 10% more than projected under the reference scenario.**

The global forest area has declined from 4.24 billion hectares in 1990 to 4.06 billion hectares in 2015 (FAO, 2020). There is good reason to believe that this declining trend could be halted, and even reversed in some regions. This view is consistent with recently adopted goals and initiatives by many countries, notably the UN Strategic Plan for Forests 2017-2030. It is plausible that changing demographics, rising global incomes, and evolving public sentiment about forests and their many benefits may result in increased investment in forest planting (Nepal *et al.*, 2019a). A projected increase in forest area may also happen as a result of countries' efforts to cut carbon emissions under the Paris Climate Agreement and work towards the UN Sustainable Development Goals (SDGs) (Freer-Smith *et al.*, 2019). The Bonn Challenge is a global initiative with just such an objective, aiming to bring 150 million hectares of degraded and deforested landscapes into restoration by 2020 and 350 million hectares by 2030. Within the UNECE region, the new EU Forest Strategy, at present under discussion, along with several other forest-relevant policy instruments could bring about policy changes that would encourage forest expansion in Europe (European Commission, 2013).

The High Forest Area (HFA) scenario projected increases in planted and natural forests, resulting in greater forest growing stock in all countries and explored the possible consequences for the forest sector as a whole.

Global **industrial roundwood** production and consumption were 40 million m$^3$ (or 2%) higher in 2040 than in the reference scenario, the natural result of a projected roundwood price that was 3% lower. Production of roundwood in the UNECE region increased by 24 million m$^3$, with the largest increases in Europe-EU, North America and the Russian Federation. The UNECE region consumed 41 million m$^3$ more roundwood in 2040 than in the reference scenario. Higher consumption than the projected production quantities resulted in lower net exports of roundwood from the UNECE region.

There were similar effects on the UNECE region **sawnwood** sector. However, the projected price decline for sawnwood was smaller (2%), and production increased more than consumption, leading to higher net exports of 13 million m$^3$ from the UNECE region. The effects on the panels sector were smaller. The effect of increasing forest stock on the paper sector was very slight in the UNECE region.

Table 3.4 provides an overview on the main outcomes of the scenario.

### 3.5.2 *Increased planted forest area outside the UNECE region*

***What if...***

***there was a rapid increase in forest growing stocks, resulting from increased planted forest outside the UNECE region?***

(Assessment through literature review)

In many countries over many years, there have been programmes to increase the area of planted forests, often to produce

roundwood at competitive prices, although other objectives, such as preventing desertification have also played a role. Plantations are producing an ever-greater share of the world's industrial wood output. The reference scenario projects that the area of planted forests will increase, but this section examines, on the basis of a literature review, possible consequences of a growth in the area of planted forests.

A recently published paper by Nepal *et al.* (2019b) described the effects of global increases in planted forests. Using the GFPM, the model simulated the changes in global forest area under SSP1-SSP5, for the period from 2015 to 2070, with and without planted forests. Under the SSP2 scenario (with extra planted forests), there was little change in the area of planted forests in the UNECE region, but a more substantial change in the rest of the world. 77% of the projected global expansion in planted area by 2040 (81 million ha) occurred outside the UNECE region (63 million ha).

Nepal *et al.* (2019b) found that global forest growing stock under the planted forest version of the GFPM would be 2% higher by 2040, than in the base scenario without extra planted forests. The overall effect of increased planted forests would be to generate prices for industrial roundwood inputs and all derived wood products lower than in the base scenario. By 2040, the difference would be less than 10%. Due to the lower prices, global production and consumption, for all products would be higher in 2040 and beyond.

The authors report no change in industrial roundwood production in Europe under the planted forest version of GFPM compared to the base version. Effects on other world regions varied substantially, with lower production in North America and South America and higher production in Africa and Asia.

### 3.5.3 *Increased natural disturbances*

**What if...**
***natural disturbances in forests were to be become more frequent and severe?***
(Assessment through literature review)

Natural disturbances such as wildfires, insect epidemics or pathogens, storms and droughts, are influenced by environmental factors, forest history and forest management. They affect supply and demand of forest products, as well as forest conditions (e.g. Holmes *et al.* 2008). Climate change is expected to result in increased frequency and severity of such future events (section 4.2.3 has more detail).

Forest disturbances tend to have short-term effects on forest product markets, mostly at the regional/national level, and much less frequently with international impacts. Short-term effects may include gluts of timber from salvage harvesting, which may drive down roundwood prices temporarily. In the longer-term, reduced forest growing stock may drive up prices, affecting production for decades in the affected regions (Prestemon and Holmes, 2008).

Research focused on the United States has shown that even the most damaging hurricanes have spatially limited, though temporally extended, impacts on production, consumption, prices, and economic welfare (Prestemon and Holmes, 2000, 2004). Simulation studies on the market effects of wildfires, imply significant effects on forest growing stock and wood product markets (Prestemon *et al.*, 2006). Similar studies of bark beetle epidemics have shown regional impacts that are similar to those caused by hurricanes (Holmes, 1991; Schwab *et al.*, 2009; Thom *et al.*, 2013). The provincial economy of British Columbia (Canada) is estimated to have suffered a long-term welfare loss of CAN$90 billion, as a result of the mountain pine beetle outbreak (Corbett *et al.*, 2016).

Natural disturbances are to a large extent unpredictable. These hampers long-term projections of their effects on market variables. The market effects of disturbances are not directly modelled in the GFPM. There are, however, some general assumptions that can be made about the possible effects of disturbances over the next 25 years on the UNECE region's forest products markets:

(i) Markets will always contain an unpredictable proportion of roundwood from salvage operations.

(ii) Salvage timber will tend to drive down roundwood prices in the short-term.

(iii) Where disturbances kill a significant proportion of standing timber, tight supply will likely cause long-term price increases.

(iv) The effects of disturbances on forest growing stock and national or regional industrial roundwood prices may be profound, making it important to explore forest dynamics models at those scales.

(v) Where disturbance is extensive, market effects may transmit internationally.

(vi) In a similar fashion, significant tree mortality in smaller countries may also have market impacts that extend beyond national borders.

At present, and pending further research, the future impacts of disturbances on global markets due to climate change are unknown. They might lead to new market impacts never experienced before, diminishing the reliability of the past as a guide for how markets will respond.

## 3.6 Increased barriers to international trade in forest products

**KEY QUESTION:**

***What if there were significant restrictions to trade in forest products?***
(Assessment through literature review)

A final question, not specifically tied to structural changes in supply or demand, called for an assessment of how increased trade barriers might affect forest products markets. After a long period when trade restrictions were steadily dismantled, the UNECE region has witnessed higher tariffs since 2017, with the United States as a central focus. As the largest producer of forest products in the world, there are large bilateral flows in forest products between the United States and Canada, which is the world's second largest producer. Both countries trade extensively with Europe and other countries of the UNECE region. Higher tariffs have impacted these trade flows. Studies that analyse the impacts of tariffs imposed by the United States reveal the possible future impacts of sustained, higher tariffs on forest products trade in the UNECE region.

Buongiorno and Johnston (2018) modelled the effects of trade barriers using the Global Forest Products Model, the same model employed for this Outlook. Although their study was limited to quantifying the effects of simulated trade friction associated only with the United States, the study is informative in revealing how such barriers, involving the world's largest timber producer and consumer, could lead to pan-UNECE and global production, consumption, price, and trade effects.

The study considered two simulations. The first simulated the effects of higher import tariffs levied by the United States (alone) against its trading partners. The second simulated the effect of these tariffs, in combination with retaliatory tariffs by the trading partners against the United States.

With higher import tariffs implemented by the United States, but no retaliatory measures, the welfare of producers in the United States rises but by less than the losses experienced by consumers in the United States, due to higher domestic prices and lower consumption. Outside the United States, producers lose more than consumers gain by paying lower prices and consuming more.

However, when the effects of retaliatory measures were added, the results within the United States were reversed, with the welfare of consumers in the United States rising due to lower prices and higher consumption, but their gains were outweighed by domestic producers' losses. The rest of the world saw decreases in consumer welfare which were greater than producer welfare increases, also a net loss Such a scenario of trade measures and counter-measures would reduce the total welfare (producer and consumer surplus) of most countries.

While some of the impacts highlighted by the authors are dependent on the countries most directly involved in any trade barrier or other trade measure (in this case the United States), the results are indicative of what such a volley of trade measures could mean for forest product markets on a global basis. It is noteworthy that in each scenario, even in the same country, there are winners and losers of trade disputes.

Non-tariff barriers, in the forms of quotas, embargoes, sanctions, or export bans, can also impact the forest sector. Measures by individual countries or trade blocs that may be categorized as non-tariff barriers are often a source of trade disputes. Environmental policies, or phytosanitary controls that are designed to prevent transfer of exotic pests and disease across borders may be viewed as non-tariff barriers (Li *et al.*, 2007). While their use may be conditionally allowed under the provisions of the World Trade Organization (World Trade Organization, 2020), they do have real impacts on international trade and are sometimes the source of trade disputes (FAO, 2005). For the forest sector, the effects of such measures are to raise global timber prices, increase consumer expenditures, and to limit production and overall trade. Specific impacts will vary widely depending on which countries are involved, the targeted products and the nature of the measures put in place. This study did not specifically model the effects of such barriers, nor was it able to judge whether or not such barriers would be more or less common in the future.

## 3.7 Data for GFPM scenarios presented in the chapter

This section presents in tabular form the main features of the scenarios prepared for the outlook study. Tables with more detail, notably by subregion, and with percentage differences may be found in the full paper.

**TABLE 3.1 GFPM projected differences in the production, consumption, net exports, prices of wood products, and forest growing stock by 2040** (projected values in 2040 in China-High Wood Consumption scenario minus reference projected values)

| | Production | Consumption | Net exports | Price[1] | Forest growing stock |
|---|---|---|---|---|---|
| | *million cubic metres* | *million cubic metres* | *million cubic metres* | *$/cubic metres* | *million cubic metres* |
| **Industrial roundwood** | | | | | |
| UNECE region | 126.4 | 98.1 | 28.3 | na | -512.3 |
| China | 96.4 | 146.2 | -49.8 | 26.6 | -1712.2 |
| World | 270.7 | 270.7 | 0 | 10.2 | -2439.2 |
| **Sawnwood** | | | | | |
| UNECE region | 51.3 | -4.6 | 55.9 | na | |
| China | 30.4 | 103.9 | -73.5 | 22.7 | |
| World | 96.8 | 96.8 | 0 | 22.7 | |
| **Panels[2]** | | | | | |
| UNECE region | 2.5 | -3.8 | 6.3 | na | |
| China | 118.8 | 128.6 | -9.8 | 29.3 | |
| World | 123.0 | 123.0 | 0 | 13.8 | |
| **Paper & paperboard[3]** | *million tonnes* | *million tonnes* | *million tonnes* | *$/tonne* | |
| UNECE region | -0.6 | -1.2 | 0.6 | na | |
| China | -0.5 | -0.6 | 0.1 | 1.9 | |
| World | -2.6 | -2.6 | 0 | 8.1 | |

**Notes:** [1] Prices for panels represent the average of prices for plywood, particle board, and fibreboard. Prices for paper and paperboard represent the average of prices for newsprint, printing and writing paper, and other paper and paperboard.
[2] Production, consumption and net export values for panels represent the sum of values for plywood, particle board, and fibreboard.
[3] Production, consumption and net export values for paper and paperboard represent the sum of values for newsprint, printing and writing paper, and other paper and paperboard.
**Source:** GFPM projections.

**TABLE 3.2 GFPM projected differences in the production, consumption, net exports, prices of wood products, and forest growing stock by 2040** (projected values in 2040 in Europe-High Wood Consumption scenario minus reference projected values)

| | Production | Consumption | Net exports | Price[1] | Forest growing stock |
|---|---|---|---|---|---|
| | *million cubic metres* | *million cubic metres* | *million cubic metres* | *$/cubic metres* | *million cubic metres* |
| **Industrial roundwood** | | | | | |
| Europe-EU | 22.1 | 46.3 | -24.2 | na | -262.7 |
| Russian Federation | 6.5 | -19.7 | 26.2 | 1.9 | -103.9 |
| North America | 20.6 | 19.1 | 1.6 | na | -175.0 |
| UNECE region | 53.6 | 52.7 | 0.9 | na | -580.5 |
| World | 90.4 | 90.4 | 0 | 3.9 | -924.3 |
| **Sawnwood** | | | | | |
| Europe-EU | 28.2 | 56.0 | -27.9 | na | |
| Russian Federation | -9.6 | 5.9 | -15.6 | 4.9 | |
| North America | 8.2 | -0.8 | 9.1 | na | |
| UNECE region | 31.9 | 65.9 | -34.0 | na | |
| World | 63.9 | 63.9 | 0 | 4.8 | |
| **Panels[2]** | | | | | |
| Europe-EU | 8.2 | 14.5 | -6.3 | na | |
| Russian Federation | 1.6 | 2.6 | -1.0 | 3.8 | |
| North America | 4.3 | 0.3 | 4.0 | na | |
| UNECE region | 15.6 | 19.5 | -3.9 | na | |
| World | 16.2 | 16.2 | 0 | 4.7 | |
| **Paper & paperboard[3]** | *million tonnes* | *million tonnes* | *million tonnes* | *$/tonne* | |
| Europe-EU | -0.8 | -0.3 | -0.5 | na | |
| Russian Federation | -0.2 | 0 | -0.1 | 4.7 | |
| North America | -0.2 | -0.2 | 0.1 | na | |
| UNECE region | -1.2 | -1.2 | -0.6 | na | |
| World | -1.3 | -1.3 | 0 | 3.4 | |

**Notes:** [1] Prices for panels represent the average of prices for plywood, particle board, and fibreboard. Paper prices are average prices for newsprint, printing and writing paper, and other paper and paperboard.

[2] Production, consumption and net export values for panels represent the sum of values for plywood, particle board, and fibreboard.

[3] Production, consumption and net export values for paper and paperboard are the sum of newsprint, printing and writing paper, and other paper and paperboard.

**Source:** GFPM projections.

**TABLE 3.3 GFPM projected differences in production, consumption, net exports, prices of wood products, and forest growing stock by 2040** (projected values in 2040 in Textile-High Wood Fibre Consumption scenario minus projected values in the reference scenario)

| | Production | Consumption | Net exports | Price[1] | Forest growing stock |
|---|---|---|---|---|---|
| | *million cubic metres* | *million cubic metres* | *million cubic metres* | *$/cubic metres* | *million cubic metres* |
| **Industrial roundwood** | | | | | |
| Europe-EU | 13.5 | 18.1 | -4.6 | na | -144.9 |
| Russian Federation | 5.3 | -11.5 | 16.9 | 1.6 | -56.1 |
| North America | 28.8 | 28 | 0.8 | na | -260.4 |
| UNECE region | 50.9 | 40.8 | 10.1 | na | -484.5 |
| World | 81.4 | 81.4 | 0 | 3.1 | -768.3 |
| **Sawnwood** | | | | | |
| Europe-EU | -10.4 | -0.6 | -9.8 | na | |
| Russian Federation | -7.3 | -0.1 | -7.2 | 4.0 | |
| North America | -11 | -1 | -9.9 | na | |
| UNECE region | -26.4 | -1.9 | -24.5 | na | |
| World | -3.5 | -3.5 | 0 | 3.9 | |
| **Panels[2]** | | | | | |
| Europe-EU | -1.3 | -0.5 | -0.8 | na | |
| Russian Federation | -0.1 | -0.1 | 0 | 3.0 | |
| North America | -1.3 | -0.5 | -0.8 | na | |
| UNECE region | -2 | -1.3 | -0.6 | na | |
| World | -3.9 | -3.9 | 0 | 3.4 | |
| **Paper & paperboard[3]** | *million tonnes* | *million tonnes* | *million tonnes* | *$/tonne* | |
| Europe-EU | -0.9 | 9.8 | 2.0 | na | |
| Russian Federation | -0.2 | -0.3 | 1.8 | 49.4 | |
| North America | 7.8 | 16.2 | 11.6 | na | |
| UNECE region | 6.1 | 24.8 | 18.0 | na | |
| World | 1.2 | 51.5 | 0.0 | 83.4 | |

**Notes:** [1] Prices for panels represent the average of prices for plywood, particle board, and fibreboard, and prices for paper and paperboard represent the average of prices for newsprint, printing and writing paper, and other paper and paperboard.

[2] Production, consumption and net export values for panels represent the sum of values for plywood, particle board, and fibreboard.

[3] Production, consumption and net export values for paper and paperboard are the sum of newsprint, printing and writing paper, and other paper and paperboard.

**Source:** GFPM projections.

**TABLE 3.4 GFPM projected differences in production, consumption, net exports, prices of wood products, and forest growing stock by 2040** (projected values in 2040 in High Forest Area scenario minus projected values in the reference scenario)

| | Production | Consumption | Net exports | Price[1] | Forest growing stock |
|---|---|---|---|---|---|
| | *million cubic metres* | *million cubic metres* | *million cubic metres* | *$/cubic metres* | *million cubic metres* |
| **Industrial roundwood** | | | | | |
| Europe-EU | 9.4 | 12.4 | -3.0 | na | 4153 |
| Russian Federation | 6.7 | 10.7 | -4.0 | -1.9 | 8,673 |
| North America | 7.4 | 18.2 | -10.9 | na | 9,578 |
| UNECE region | 23.9 | 40.6 | -16.7 | na | 23,852 |
| World | 39.7 | 39.7 | 0 | -3.6 | 56,544 |
| **Sawnwood** | | | | | |
| Europe-EU | 2.1 | 0.8 | 1.3 | na | |
| Russian Federation | 4.7 | 0.1 | 4.6 | -4.6 | |
| North America | 9.4 | 0.9 | 8.5 | na | |
| UNECE region | 14.9 | 2.0 | 12.9 | na | |
| World | 4.3 | 4.3 | 0 | -4.7 | |
| **Panels[2]** | | | | | |
| Europe-EU | 2.2 | 0.8 | 1.4 | na | |
| Russian Federation | 0 | 0.1 | -0.1 | -3.7 | |
| North America | -0.7 | 0.6 | -1.2 | na | |
| UNECE region | 1.9 | 1.8 | 0.1 | na | |
| World | 4.9 | 4.9 | 0 | -4.3 | |
| **Paper & paperboard[3]** | *million tonnes* | *million tonnes* | *million tonnes* | *$/tonne* | |
| Europe-EU | -0.3 | 0.3 | -0.7 | na | |
| Russian Federation | 0.1 | 0 | 0 | -4.0 | |
| North America | 0.6 | 0.3 | 0.2 | na | |
| UNECE region | 0.3 | 0.7 | -0.5 | na | |
| World | 1.6 | 1.6 | 0 | -4.1 | |

**Notes:** [1] Prices for panels represent the average of prices for plywood, particle board, and fibreboard, and prices for paper and paperboard represent the average of prices for newsprint, printing and writing paper, and other paper and paperboard.

[2] Production, consumption and net export values for panels represent the sum of values for plywood, particle board, and fibreboard.

[3] Production, consumption and net export values for paper and paperboard represent the sum of values for newsprint, printing and writing paper, and other paper and paperboard.

**Source:** GFPM projections.

# 4 Climate change

## Key points

- Climate change impacts on forests will be profound: extended, warmer growing seasons and higher levels of atmospheric $CO_2$ might enhance productivity in parts of the UNECE region, but more frequent and severe events, such as drought or storms could increase the likelihood of increased GHG emissions for instance from fire, outbreaks of pests, and disease.

- Forests help to mitigate climate change and the study projects rising carbon storage, with UNECE region forests being a projected net carbon sink of 1.5 billion $tCO_2e$ per year over the period of this study.

- Natural disturbances, exacerbated by climate change, are a challenge for forest management, damaging forest ecosystems and wood markets, as well as causing increased carbon emissions.

- The current disturbance effects on carbon flows may be as large as the net carbon sink of forests in the UNECE region. Therefore, forest management strategies for climate change mitigation may consider taking forest disturbances into account. Adaptation and mitigation measures should ideally be considered together.

- Increasing global forest area by 10% by 2040 would sequester an additional 1.43 billion $tCO_2e$ per year in the UNECE region.

- Increased wood removals to substitute fossil-based alternatives in textile manufacture and wood construction were projected to be nearly carbon neutral, as changes in the forest biomass stock counterbalance the avoided emissions.

- Adaptive management of forests, which may be reactive or proactive, each with its own type of risk, will be crucial to maintain multiple functions of forests.

- Climate change impacts might also present windows of opportunity for adaptation by diversifying forest structure and species mix.

## 4.1 Introduction

This chapter addresses the key questions about the possible consequences for the forest sector of climate change and questions related to climate change mitigation and substitution. It summarises a full academic study which is being published separately, titled "The outlook for UNECE forest sector in a changing climate: a contribution to the Forest Sector Outlook Study 2020-2040" in the series of UNECE/FAO Discussion Papers. This chapter summarises the full analysis, focusing more on the results than on the methodology. Readers who need more information on the sources, methods and results should consult the full study.

Earth's climate has changed appreciably since the beginning of the industrial age. Atmospheric levels of $CO_2$ have risen significantly. Surface temperatures over much of the northern hemisphere increased by more than 1°C between 1901 and 2012, and by more than 2°C in large parts of Canada and the Russian Federation (IPCC, 2014). Boreal forests have experienced the largest temperature increases, in comparison to other forest biomes (Gauthier *et al.*, 2015). These warming trends are projected to continue, though the size of the increase will vary according to the emission pathway.

Projected trends for precipitation are much more uncertain. Projected precipitation varies widely across the UNECE region, depending on which pathway or global climate model is considered.

Substantial seasonality is expected, as well as increased frequency of extreme climatic events in response to climate change. Winter temperatures are expected to rise faster than summer temperatures, with larger changes at higher latitudes. Winters are expected to be wetter, with dryer summers leading to drought conditions in some regions, coinciding with high water demand by agriculture and cities (Lindner *et al.*, 2014). There is an increasing probability of temperature extremes, with excessive summer heat.

Climate change will impact forest ecosystems in a variety of ways. This chapter provides a comprehensive overview of how UNECE forests might be affected in different regions, how forests might contribute to climate mitigation, and how forest management may need to adapt to changing conditions.

## 4.2 Climate change impacts on forests

Trees are long-lived. Their productivity and health reflect weather and site conditions, past site development, management history and disturbances. Consequently, understanding how climate change will affect forests is complicated. Changing temperatures, precipitation and atmospheric $CO_2$ concentrations are likely to influence growth rates directly, quite often by enhancing photosynthesis and indirectly by changing long-term growing conditions and forest dynamics. In addition to these gradual changes, climate change is affecting the frequency and severity of natural disturbances and extreme events. All these factors will strongly influence tree species distribution, forest health, productivity, function, and ecosystem services.

This section looks at how climate-induced changes in growing conditions could affect forest productivity and tree species distribution. It also examines the incidence of extreme events and forest disturbances, and the effects of climate change on harvesting conditions. Finally, it presents an initial analysis of how projected changes in net primary productivity could influence forest product markets.

### 4.2.1 *Climate change impacts on forest productivity*

Forest productivity is mainly influenced by temperature, precipitation and atmospheric $CO_2$ concentrations, as well as nitrogen deposition and land and forest management. Enhanced photosynthetic activity has helped to green many parts of the world, including northern Europe and the Russian Federation (Zhu *et al.*, 2015). This is the result of increasing levels of atmospheric $CO_2$, longer growing seasons and warmer springs.

Climate change and nitrogen deposition appear to have contributed to increasing forest productivity in Central Europe (Pretzsch *et al.*, 2013) and in the United States (McMahon *et al.*, 2010). In Canada, positive and negative climate-induced growth changes cancel each other out (Girardin *et al.*, 2016).

In the Mediterranean area, there is contrasting evidence of growth increase and decrease depending on tree species, competition, site productivity and local climatic conditions (Sarris *et al.*, 2011; Martin-Benito *et al.*, 2011; Tegel *et al.*, 2014; Charru *et al.*, 2017). However, it is highly uncertain whether the strong positive effects of increasing atmospheric $CO_2$ on forest productivity will persist in the future, or be limited, either by physiological constraints (de Boer *et al.*, 2011) or by the availability of phosphorus and nitrogen (Hungate, 2003; Norby *et al.*, 2010). Nevertheless, there is some prospect for increasing forest productivity in many temperate and boreal forests of the UNECE region, as projected by process-based forest models (Reyer *et al.*, 2014; Reyer *et al.*, 2015; Friend *et al.*, 2014; Ito *et al.*, 2020). Some studies suggest that growth increases might not occur, if water availability restricts forest carbon accumulation (Kint *et al.*, 2012; Sperry *et al.*, 2019), if growth increases in spring are compensated for by growth reductions later in the growing season (Buermann *et al.*, 2018), or if climate change increases background mortality in forest stands (Bugmann & Bigler, 2011; Yu *et al.*, 2019). Mediterranean forests are already limited by water availability and at greater risk of climate-induced productivity losses (FAO & Plan Bleu, 2018). Furthermore, enhanced productivity does not necessarily produce high-quality timber, as faster growth may lead to lower wood quality (Box 4.1).

### *4.2.2 Climate change impacts on species distribution*

Changes in growing conditions not only affect forest productivity, but also the distribution range of tree species. The concept of the fundamental niche describes the range of environmental conditions a species could theoretically occupy under stable conditions. The area actually occupied, the realized niche, is often smaller due to the presence of competition with other species and natural barriers (Griesemer, 1994).[10] Forests that move outside their fundamental niche risk productivity loss, reduced resilience, or replacement by other vegetation types (Dyderski *et al.*, 2018; Reyer *et al.*, 2014). With climate change, shifts have been observed at the leading edges of species distributions. Species expand into habitats that now increasingly provide the required environmental resources to sustain growth and competitiveness (Lindner *et al.*, 2014). As climate change progresses, species range and their associated forest types may move towards the poles and higher altitudes (Meier *et al.*, 2012). This would have strong implications for the profitability of commercial forestry, and the main tree species grown in Europe (Hanewinkel *et al.*, 2013).

10 Forest management relies on this concept by cultivating economically important tree species beyond the realized, but still within the fundamental niche, which requires the continuous removal of competitors.

Species migration trends have been observed throughout the UNECE region. In Siberia, the slow migration of evergreen conifer species into current larch habitat has been reported (Kharuk *et al.*, 2007). In North America, temperate deciduous tree species have migrated into the boreal zone (Boisvert-Marsh *et al.*, 2014). At higher elevations in southern Europe, holm oak is replacing beech (Penuelas *et al.*, 2007). These migration trends are consistent with projected shifts in species ranges, highlighting that, for many species, the rate of migration may not keep pace with changing climatic conditions (Delzon *et al.*, 2013). Generally, distributions of species, especially at the rear edges of their range, are often susceptible to disturbances like drought, pathogens and insects.

**BOX 4.1**

**Climate change impacts on wood quality**

Increased forest productivity may produce wider growth rings and longer fibres, which will influence wood quality in terms of strength and chemical properties (Mitchell, 1961). Climatic variables strongly influence characteristics like strength and stiffness, which are affected by wood density (Zhu *et al.*, 2015). While growth rates in Central Europe accelerated throughout the 20th century, wood density declined (Pretzsch *et al.*, 2018). Warm spring conditions led to higher proportions of low-density early wood in annual growth rings. Lower wood density can reduce mechanical stability, increasing the risk of snow damage (Peltola *et al.*, 1999) and wind damage (Meyer *et al.*, 2008).

Water stress negatively affects radial tree growth. A higher incidence of drought may produce heterogeneous tree-ring patterns. Decreasing homogeneity and trends in wood density are likely to cause problems for use in construction and furniture (Lachenbruch *et al.*, 2010). In a few cases, lower wood density may have a positive effect, for instance for sliced-veneer production (Zhang *et al.*, 1993).

### *4.2.3 Climate change impacts on natural disturbances*

Disturbances such as fire, windthrow and insect outbreaks are a natural component of forest dynamics, disrupting ecosystem structure, composition and function. In unmanaged systems, disturbances create a heterogeneous landscape. Disturbances not only alter resource availability but also promote forest rejuvenation, which is crucial for adaptation to environmental changes, including those linked to climate change. Disturbances over large areas have a significant impact on forests (Seidl *et al.*, 2017) and carbon storage (McNulty 2002, Seidl *et al.*, 2014).

Forest disturbances have been increasing in frequency and severity since the early 1970s (Schelhaas, Nabuurs, & Schuck, 2003; Seidl, 2014). This trend is expected to continue (Chi *et al.*, 2019; Seidl & Rammer, 2017). A combination of changes in forest structure, forest management, and climate are the main causes of increased disturbance (Seidl *et al.*, 2017; Abatzoglou & Williams, 2016; Sommerfeld *et al.*, 2018). Disturbance agents rarely occur alone, often acting in combination. For example, a storm may leave many dead trees, which provide a suitable environment for bark beetles or fuel for forest fires. How disturbances interact very much depends on the forest condition and climate zones (Dale *et al.*, 2010; Reyer *et al.*, 2017). The following sections briefly review the situation and outlook or each disturbance type.

### Wind

#### Factors influencing wind damage

The susceptibility of trees and forest stands to wind damage is strongly linked to wind speed, duration, and gustiness, and varies with tree species, height, stem density, and the presence or absence of gaps in the canopy from previous disturbances. Other factors include stand location in relation to prevailing wind direction, past forest management, such as thinning and final cutting, and the soil type and topography (Hanewinkel *et al.*, 2014). Seasonality is also important. Resistance to wind damage depends on tree height, stem diameter, rooting system, foliage, and crown development (Hale *et al.*, 2012). By promoting root and crown development, thinning may make stands more resistant to wind damage, although there is often a short-lived increased risk of wind damage after thinnings as canopy roughness temporarily increases.

There have been several recent examples of major wind damage in UNECE region forests. Storm Gudrun in Sweden in 2005 caused windfall of 75 million $m^3$ within hours (Kauppi *et al.*, 2018). Hurricanes Katrina and Rita damaged 2.23 million hectares of forests along the east coast of the United States in 2005 (Stanturf *et al.*, 2007). In 1989, Hurricane Hugo caused damage valued at more than $1,500 million to forests in South Carolina, with measurable economic effects on timber markets over more than two decades (Prestemon and Holmes, 2000, 2004).

Uprooted but unbroken trees can still yield sawlogs, but where stems have been snapped the merchantable value is reduced significantly, and salvage harvesting may only be possible in restricted time windows (Prestemon and Holmes, 2004). Uprooted trees carry a higher risk of injury to forest workers and raise the cost of removal (Kärhä *et al.*, 2018).

#### Outlook for wind damage

Extra-tropical storms have increased in frequency and intensity, a trend that is expected to intensify with ongoing climate change (Ullbrich *et al.*, 2009). The typical storm tracks of hurricanes affecting eastern North America may be altered and storms are projected to reach the coasts of western Europe with increasing frequency over coming decades (Haarsma *et al.*, 2013).

Predictions about damage to forests on both sides of the Atlantic resulting from future storm patterns remain uncertain. Current global climate models struggle to predict regional wind speeds and the associated risks of storms. Projections of increased storm impacts are based mainly on indirect effects (Lindner & Rummukainen, 2013). Enhanced forest productivity is likely to increase tree heights and stand densities, which may make stands more vulnerable to wind damage (Reyer *et al.*, 2017). Higher winter precipitation and shorter duration of frozen soils under a warming climate may reduce stand stability, especially in boreal forests, where winter temperatures are projected to increase the most (Usbeck *et al.*, 2010).

### Drought

#### Factors influencing drought damage

Trees respond to dry and hot weather by shutting down photosynthesis to conserve water and prevent xylem cavitation – the loss of conductivity within tree vessels (Li *et al.*, 2015). Consecutive droughts impair tree health, reducing growth and weakening natural defence mechanisms, increasing susceptibility to storm, fire, pathogens, and insects (Lindner *et al.*, 2014). Reduced resin production for instance, weakens a tree's defences against insect attacks (McDowell et al, 2011). Reduced growth also limits root growth, potentially destabilizing the tree and lowering resistance to windthrow (Zhou *et al.*, 2018). The risk of fire may increase, as dried wood on the forest floor ignites more easily and will burn at higher temperatures than moist wood. In the Northern Hemisphere, defoliation and drought-induced mortality has increased over a wide variety of tree species (Settele *et al.* 2014)

#### Outlook for drought damage

Droughts have increased in number, severity and duration since the beginning of the 20th century (IPCC, 2013). Climate models project a possible doubling in drought occurrence for many UNECE subregions (McDowell *et al.*, 2018). Drought length and severity are projected to increase with lower summer precipitation and higher evapotranspiration (Dai, 2013). This would cause more of the type of damage described above.

### Fire

#### Recent developments

Fire is the primary driver of forest dynamics in boreal and Mediterranean forests (Boulanger *et al.*, 2013). This is also the case for other forest types, such as those in the west of North America. Historically, fire also played a role in temperate forest dynamics (Adamek *et al.*, 2018).

Since 1990, the area in the Mediterranean basin affected by fire has been decreasing, except for Portugal: (San-Miguel-Ayanz *et al.*, 2018), causing an annual loss of about 1.5 billion euros (San-Miguel-Ayanz and Camia, 2010). The young and largely unmanaged forests resulting from afforestation and natural extension contain high fuel loads and connectivity over large areas, which create favourable conditions for rapid and large spread of wildfires. The cultivation of fire-prone trees, such as eucalyptus and some pines, has increased fire risk (Gonçalves and Sousa, 2017). Wildfires show large year-to-year variation in frequency and scale: Wildfires have been increasing in other parts of Europe since 1990, particularly in Germany, Poland and Sweden.

In Canada and the United States, wildfires have been trending upwards since at least the mid-1980s. Between 2000 to 2018, the area burned rose to 5.3 million hectares (National Interagency Fire Center 2019a, Natural Resources Canada 2019). This not only results in higher carbon and other emissions but adds greatly to the cost of suppression - $2.1billion/year for federal agencies in the United States alone (National Interagency Fire Center 2019b, United States Department of Commerce 2019). Particles from fires spread to populated areas throughout North America, causing significant health effects (Kochi *et al.*, 2010, Fann *et al.*, 2018).

Fire is the main cause of forest disturbance in the Russian Federation. Between 1998 and 2013, fires in the Russian Federation have affected between 8 million and 11 million hectares annually, of which 5 million hectares were forested (Schaphoff *et al.*, 2016). Satellite imaging showed that between 2001 and 2019, fires affected between 2 million and 11 million hectares of forest, yearly averaging 5.6 million hectares (Leskinen *et al.*, 2020). Despite high year-to-year variation, the area burnt in Russian forests is increasing. The distribution of fire is uneven, however. While climate change may have a role in the increasing incidence of fires, there is also a strong socioeconomic/political element. The transition away from a centrally planned economy in the Russian Federation has led to an increasing area of abandoned farmland and reduced numbers of forest managers and forest firefighters leading to less efficient forest protection systems (Isaev and Korovin, 2013, Flannigan *et al.*, 2009).

### *Outlook for fire damage*

Rising temperatures and shifts in precipitation cause more frequent dry weather. Together with larger quantities of fuel wood and higher lightning activity, these are expected to increase the numbers, size, and intensity of fires (Whitman *et al.*, 2015; Turco *et al.*, 2019). The changes in fire dynamics caused by climate change adversely affect the recovery of forest structure and composition, hampering the provision of forest ecosystem services (Halofsky *et al.*, 2020).

## Insects and pathogens

### *Recent developments*

Warmer, drier conditions in recent years have favoured the spread of bark beetles. Taken together with a reduction in the natural ability of trees to resist attack, this has resulted in extensive and extended infestations, especially in Central Europe and North America where even-aged, largely conifer stands have provided an ideal habitat for bark beetles. In the dry European summer of 2018, bark beetles were able to complete a third reproduction cycle, causing unprecedented outbreaks in Central Europe. In the Czech Republic, the volume of infested timber equaled the scheduled annual harvest of 17 million $m^3$ (Ekolyst, 2019). In Germany, over one-third of the harvested volume in 2018 was of salvaged spruce timber (Destatis, 2019; Destatis, 2020).

In Canada, outbreaks of mountain pine beetle have affected over 18 million hectares of forests in British Columbia and Alberta since the 1990s. Peaking in 2004, it was estimated to have destroyed 752 million $m^3$ of merchantable timber by 2017 (Natural Resources Canada 2018). The economic impacts of bark beetle epidemics in this area are also potentially huge (Holmes 1991, Prestemon *et al.*, 2013).

The Siberian silk moth is one of the most damaging insect pests affecting boreal forests. Rising temperatures have allowed it to extend its range in the Russian Federation, and there is concern that it is spreading into northern and north eastern Siberia. It is even possible that it may spread west to Belarus and Finland (CABI, 2021). An outbreak that began in 2014 on the Yenisei plain has continued its northward spread, extending well beyond its historical northern limit (Kharuk *et al.*, 2018).

### *Outlook for insects and pathogens*

Climate change directly influences the survival and metabolic rate of insects and pathogens. Warmer and wetter climate conditions are expected to increase the activity and abundance of pathogens (Müller *et al.*, 2014). A warmer and drier future will enhance insect reproduction and survival rates (Seidl *et al.*, 2017). Climate change will also affect the abundance, diversity and growth rates of host trees and thereby their capacity to resist. Recurring drought, for example, may compromise host tree defences against insects, through reduced resin production (Gaylord *et al.*, 2013).

## Snow & ice

### *Recent developments*

The weight of snow and ice that accumulates on tree crowns can break branches and tree stems. In combination with a lack of frozen soil and strong winds, heavy ice and snow may even uproot trees (Gregow *et al.*, 2011). Young, unthinned stands are most likely to suffer (Paatolo, 2000). In mountainous regions, avalanches, though declining in frequency, are a continuing hazard for forests (Teich *et al.*, 2012). Between 1950 and 2000, snow-damaged timber from European forests was recorded at a mean annual volume of one million $m^3$ (Schelhaas *et al.*, 2003). Ice storms, though uncommon, have a strong impact on forests. In 2014, ice damaged an estimated 9.3 million $m^3$ of timber in Croatia and Slovenia (Nagel *et al.*, 2016). Ice storms have been a particular concern in the east of North America, where they occur more often. The 1994 Mississippi ice storm damaged 41 million $m^3$, including 18 million $m^3$ of sawtimber, a volume greater than the annual intake of the state's sawmilling sector (Irland, 2000).

#### *Outlook for damage by snow and ice*

It is difficult to assess from climate models how future changes in climate might influence the scale and frequency of such events. Snow cover in the northern hemisphere has been decreasing since the 1930s (Brown & Robinson, 2011), and it is likely this trend will continue (IPCC, 2013). Disturbances from snow and ice are therefore likely to decrease as the climate changes (Seidl. *et al.*, 2017).

### *4.2.4 Climate change impacts on harvest conditions*

#### *Climate and wood harvesting*

In boreal and cold-winter temperate forests, harvesting has traditionally been undertaken in winter when frozen soils improve the efficient operation of forest machinery, and reduce soil damage.

Wet and waterlogged soils, such as sites with deep clay or loamy soils, are much more prone to damage, which may result in reduced productivity (Toivio *et al.*, 2017). Damaged soils may also affect species compositions and forest functioning (Closset-Kopp *et al.*, 2019).

In Wisconsin, USA, a study reported that frozen ground conditions had shortened by three weeks on average since 1948, leading to a shift in harvesting of pine, rather than hardwoods and other coniferous species (Rittenhouse & Rissmann 2015).

#### *Outlook for wood harvesting conditions*

Rising winter temperatures may restrict harvesting operations by reducing the number of days when soils remain frozen (Henry, 2008, Rittenhouse & Rissmann, 2015). Excessive off-season rainfall may have a similar impact, making it difficult to continue harvesting without damaging vulnerable soils, with potentially serious consequences for timber production. As a result, Finland, for example, is facing difficulties to meet its climate mitigation targets (Lehtonen *et al.* 2019). These targets rely heavily on bioenergy from forested peatlands, where harvesting may become impossible because of shortening periods of frozen soils.

Extraction could be shifted towards summer months when soils tend to be dry, although motor manual felling during the growing season could damage and devalue timber. This is because large-crowned trees tend to splinter when in sap, reducing the volume of merchantable timber.

Damage from natural disturbance will increase harvesting costs as a consequence of greater planning effort. It will also lower efficiency due to the chaotic effects of windthrow, for example, and the higher safety standards essential under such conditions (Kärhä *et al.*, 2018).

Changing winter conditions and natural disturbance as a result of climate change might lead to a cascade of problems for commercial and pre-commercial harvesting, for all-year-round working, and for maintaining a steady labour supply. Forest managers might be able to time harvesting operations for when and where soils and species allow but harvesting operations are increasingly constrained by a shrinking winter window, salvage logging, and essential sanitary felling. Forest operations are becoming more seasonal and harvesting will become variable across the year. This will restrict employment of forest workers, create logistical challenges for wood-processing plants that rely on stable roundwood supplies, and limit opportunities to carry out pre-commercial thinning.

### *4.2.5 Forest products market impacts of climate change induced by changes in net primary productivity*

This section summarizes the simulated impacts of projected changes in forest productivity on global forest products markets. It is important to note that this modelling approach includes only changes in net primary productivity (NPP) of forests but does not include effects of disturbances other than wildfires.

Table 4.1 summarizes the relative differences for 2040 between a scenario with increased forest productivity and one without this increase, showing results for only a few countries and parameters. More complete results and information on methodology are available in the UNECE/FAO Discussion Paper "The outlook for UNECE forest sector in a changing climate: a contribution to the Forest Sector Outlook Study 2020-2040".

The modelling results suggest that climate change, in the scenario with the highest $CO_2$ concentrations, would generally increase forest productivity, reducing prices and increasing global forest product consumption and production. However, results also suggest that price declines brought about by higher global forest productivity will alter production and trade competitiveness of individual countries.

It should be noted however that this modelling was based on the highest greenhouse gas concentrations and did not take into account types of climate change impacts other than increases in productivity, although these have been shown in the previous section to have a significant influence on forest ecosystems and wood production.

**TABLE 4.1 Projected percentage differences in 2040 between scenario with forest productivity change driven by Representative Concentration Pathways 8.5 and scenario based on SSP5 without climate change effects, selected regions/countries and parameters (%)**

| | Projected Net Primary Productivity values | Price of industrial roundwood | Production of industrial roundwood | Consumption of sawnwood |
|---|---|---|---|---|
| Canada | 7 | -4.4 | 3.2 | 1.6 |
| Eastern Europe & Central Asia | -1 | na | -5.4 | 0.6 |
| Russian Federation | 3 | -2.7 | 0.1 | 1.1 |
| United States of America | 15 | -6.1 | 11.5 | 1.7 |
| Western Europe | 1 | -1.6 to -3.6 | -1.7 | 0.7 |
| World | na | -2.9 | 2.7 | 1.0 |

**Source:** GFPM projections, for methods and more detailed results see the forthcoming UNECE/FAO SP "The outlook for UNECE forest sector in a changing climate: a contribution to the Forest Sector Outlook Study 2020-2040".

## 4.3 Forest sector contribution to climate change mitigation

**KEY QUESTION:**

***How can UNECE forests and the forest sector contribute to climate change mitigation?***

Forests mitigate climate change in several ways. They take up carbon while growing and store carbon in the living biomass above and below ground, in dead wood and soils. However, forest disturbances may release large amounts of forest carbon, counterbalancing the mitigation effect (Seidl *et al.*, 2014). Harvesting trees releases part of the carbon into the atmosphere, but another part remains stored in wood products, where the lifespan may vary from days to centuries. Using wood to replace energy-intensive materials, such as concrete, steel and plastic could play a significant part in limiting emissions from fossil fuel sources. Generating energy from woody biomass instead of fossil fuels avoids the use of fossil fuels and their associated emissions. Strategies for the forest sector should consider the carbon balances of growing forests and wood products, at all stages of the cycle.

This section discusses the carbon-related aspects of the forest sector scenarios presented in chapter 3, and then presents and discusses options for improving the forest sector's contribution to climate change mitigation.

### *4.3.1 Climate change mitigation in the reference scenario*

Carbon stock in above and below ground forest biomass in the UNECE region in 2015 totaled 303 billion metric tonnes of carbon dioxide equivalent ($tCO_2e$), (Johnston *et al.*, 2019). This would translate to an estimated average carbon stock of 182 $tCO_2e$/ha. The largest stocks are located in the Russian Federation (121 billion $tCO_2e$ – 40%) and North America (130 billion $tCO_2e$ – 43%) (Figure 4.1). The average annual forest carbon sequestration rate for the whole of the UNECE region between 2015 and 2040, projected by GFPM, was 1.5 billion $tCO_2e$ per year in the reference scenario. For comparison, fossil fuel emissions in 2019 for the UNECE region were 11.4 billion $tCO_2e$. All UNECE subregions are predicted to constitute a net forest carbon sink until at least 2040. Globally, the net annual forest carbon sink was 1.2 billion $tCO_2e$ per

**FIGURE 4.1 CARBON STOCK IN ABOVE- AND BELOW-GROUND FOREST BIOMASS IN THE UNECE REGION UNDER THE REFERENCE SCENARIO**

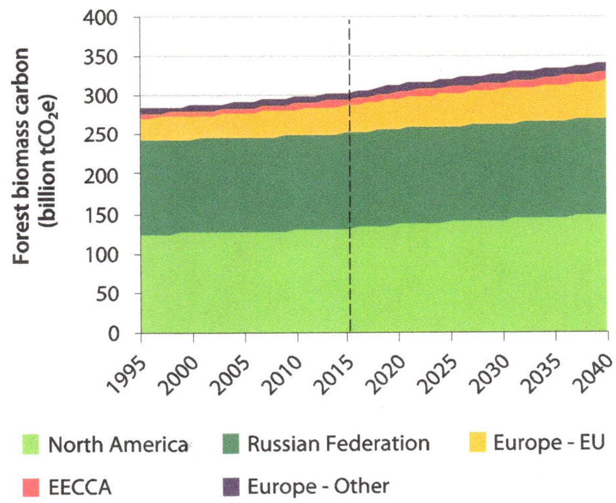


**Note:** Historical data until 2015, followed by GFPM projections until 2040.
**Source:** GFPM projections.

year: forests in Africa, Oceania and South America were all net sources of carbon.

The contribution of harvested wood products (HWP) to climate change has long been recognized and is incorporated into the annually submitted national GHG emission reports. Reporting HWP carbon storage follows the convention that carbon in the HWP pool is assigned to the country that produced the wood, rather than the country that consumed the wood product. The HWP pool may be a carbon sink or source, depending on the balance between carbon entering and leaving the pool. The manufacture of new wood products adds carbon to the HWP pool. As older products reach the end of their life, they may decay, be incinerated or landfilled, releasing carbon from the pool.

An estimated 14.3 billion $tCO_2e$ were stored in HWP in 2015 in the UNECE region. North America had the largest stocks (5.9 billion $tCO_2e$, 41%), followed by Europe-EU (5.1 billion $tCO_2e$, 36%) (Figure 4.2). Globally, in 2015, the HWP carbon pool acted as a net annual sink of 0.47 billion $tCO_2e$ per year. How the HWP sink behaves in the future will depend on the development of wood product markets (Johnston and Radeloff 2019; Pilli *et al.*, 2015). Under the projections of the reference scenario, the global annual sink is estimated to be between 0.44 and 0.63 billion $tCO_2e$ per year. In 2015, the UNECE region accounted for 24% of the global HWP sink. This share would increase to 35% in 2040. Asia, with its rapidly growing population and economic growth, accounts for 58% of the global HWP carbon sink.

**FIGURE 4.2 CARBON STOCK IN HWP IN THE UNECE REGION UNDER THE REFERENCE SCENARIO**

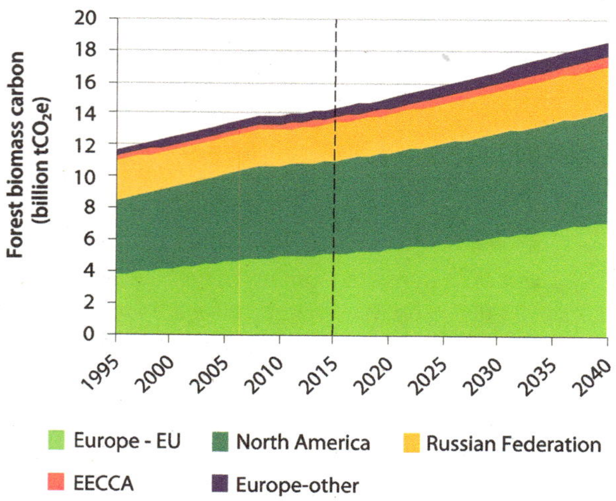


**Note:** Historical data until 2015, followed by GFPM projections until 2040.
**Source:** GFPM projections.

Projections of carbon storage in HWPs are small compared to the projections for above- and below-ground biomass carbon. The projected HWP carbon storage rate for the UNECE region would be only around 13% of the projected sequestration rate for above and below ground biomass.

### 4.3.2 *Options for increased mitigation*

The principal strategies for enhancing the forest sector's contribution to climate change mitigation are: boosting carbon storage in existing forests, reforesting degraded lands and afforesting new land, increasing the use of wood products as an alternative to carbon intensive products, thereby increasing carbon stored in HWP, and encouraging the use of sustainable woody biomass to replace non-renewable or oil based materials and energy.

Applying these strategies is not straightforward and may involve trade-offs. For instance, using more wood in manufacturing or energy may result in more intensive harvesting. This would lower forest carbon stock but would also cut carbon emissions from energy use. Conversely, harvest reductions may lead to greater forest carbon stock but could result in lower mitigation in manufacturing and energy. A mix of measures will be needed to enhance global afforestation and avoid deforestation and degradation, improved forest management to store more carbon in forests and use wood sustainably and substitute non-renewable carbon-intensive materials.

This section attempts to quantify and briefly analyse the prospects for these strategies.

#### *Potential for carbon sequestration by forest ecosystems through forest management*

Forest management measures for climate change mitigation may be broadly categorized as improving management of natural and planted forests, avoiding wood harvesting for energy production, and more active wildfire management (Griscom *et al.*, 2017). This could involve stimulating volume increment, planting faster-growing or better-adapted tree species or provenances, adopting carbon-preserving management such as continuous cover forestry or reducing harvests.

At present the forests of the UNECE region are a significant net carbon sink. However, this could change, depending on climate change and policy/management choices.

Several studies have estimated the future forest carbon sink, as well as mitigation potentials for parts of the UNECE region. These are summarised in the full paper, with some ranges and orders of magnitude in Table 4.2. Most studies have quantified only the impacts of reduced or increased harvests which increase or reduce the sink. On average, for a 10% change in harvest (up or down), the sink changes by 59 million $tCO_2e$ in the opposite direction. A conversion to

**TABLE 4.2 Future forest carbon sink, and possible impact of reducing or increasing harvest, based on FSOS modelling**

| | Reference scenario | Change if harvest decreased by 3 to 4% | Change if harvest increased by 3 to 4% |
|---|---|---|---|
| | *(Billion $tCO_2e$ per year, average 2015-2040)* | | |
| European Union | 0.47 (0.15-0.47) | 0.04 (0.04 to 0.21) | -0.02 (-0.02 to -0.1) |
| Europe Other | 0.13 (0.04 to 0.13) | 0.01 (0.01) | 0 (0) |
| Canada | -0.02 | 0.01 | -0.01 |
| USA | 0.71 (0.71 to 0.75) | 0.03 (0.03 to 0.04) | -0.02 (- 0.02 to -0.3) |

**Note:** For methodology and assumptions of FSOS scenarios, see chapter 3. Figures in brackets are the range of results from other studies, with different assumptions, methods and coverage (only one study cited for Canada). For references and more information, see the full paper.

more productive species is unlikely to have much effect until after 2040 (Nabuurs *et al.*, 2014).

Varying assessments of the Russian forest carbon sink make it challenging to assess the current carbon budget. Estimates range from 0.1 to 2.6 billion $tCO_2e$, with uncertainty about whether emissions from fire are included (estimated at 300+/-55 million $tCO_2e$ per year).

However, even if improved management and reduced harvests build up the forest carbon stock, natural disturbances can disrupt the forest carbon cycle. In the short term, natural disturbances may release large volumes of $CO_2$ although in the longer term they may help maintain the carbon sink by altering age-class distribution and introducing younger trees (Pugh *et al.*, 2019).

Discussion of the complexity of managing or expanding forest carbon while facing rising rates of natural disturbances, particularly wildfire, has focused on forests of the western United States (Sample *et al.*, 2015). In this region, estimated current rates of emission from natural disturbances, such as insects and fires, are roughly the same order of magnitude as the benefits from improved forest management. A hypothetical doubling of the effects of greater disturbance would completely offset any mitigating effect of improved forest management. Viewed globally, improved management and measures to reduce disturbances have apparently comparable effects on net carbon sequestration. However, it has so far proved difficult to demonstrate direct trade-offs between them.

Modelling the carbon mitigation potential of the United States forest sector showed that a large increase in wood removals, driven by economic and population growth, together with higher wood energy consumption, would result in United States forests becoming a carbon source after 2045 (Nepal *et al.*, 2012; Ince *et al.*, 2011). By contrast, reduced wood removals, linked to historically low wood energy consumption, are projected to increase average net carbon sequestration by 0.04 billion $tCO_2e$ per year.

Other possibilities to increase forests' contribution to climate change mitigation have also been proposed.

One approach is to institute extreme shifts in forest management, such as the absolute preservation of forests. Studies have found that this approach gives only modest mitigation potential, because increased carbon sequestration in preserved forests would be counteracted by increased harvests elsewhere. This economic "leakage" effect is caused by lower overall timber supplies driving up prices and leading to more harvesting from other forests (Nepal *et al.*, 2013).

In the Russian Federation, the potential to reduce greenhouse gas emissions from wildfires is estimated at 0.220-0.420 billion $tCO_2e$ per year (Romanovskaya *et al.*, 2019;). Furthermore, minimizing soil disturbance during logging could reduce these emissions by 0.015-0.059 billion $tCO_2e$ per year. Forest residues also play a role: current data show that wood residues from forest harvesting in the Russian Federation range from 40% to 50% of tree biomass. Reducing this could reduce emissions by 0.061–0.076 billion $tCO_2e$ per year (Romanovskaya *et al.*, 2019; Shvidenko *et al.*, 1997). However, it is unlikely that any of these options will be implemented soon and on a large scale.

### *Potential for carbon sequestration by forests through reforestation and afforestation*

Afforestation is considered an important option Research since the first IPCC special report on Land Use, Land-Use Change and Forestry in 2020 (IPCC, 2019) suggests afforestation could significantly reduce global net carbon emissions. Afforestation's ability to sequester large volumes of $CO_2$ per unit of forest area, make it an attractive option compared to other mitigation strategies. Substantial emission reductions result when models assume a commitment to substantial growth in land areas dedicated to Bioenergy and Carbon Capture and Storage (BECCS) (Popp *et al.*, 2017). In the absence of this commitment, continued emissions from fossil fuels inhibit lower net emissions. The recent IPCC Special Report considered that an expansion of global forest area by 1 billion hectares would be a cost-effective way of limiting temperature increases to 1.5°C above pre-industrial levels by 2100 (IPCC, 2018).

The High Forest Area (HFA) scenario in this study (see section 3.5.1) assumes a global forest area increase of 10% by 2040. This translates to a sizable increase in the rate of global carbon sequestration in above- and below-ground forest biomass. The additional sequestration compared to the reference scenario is 5.87 billion $tCO_2e$ per year over the period 2015-2040, of which 1.43 billion $tCO_2e$ per year for the UNECE region (Table 3.4). This strategy would make a significant contribution to global emissions compensation of close to 4%, but would require an unprecedented extra 180-320 million hectares of new plantations. This will require huge efforts to identify areas, involve landowners and local communities, introduce socio-economic incentives, and expand wood manufacturing. Only then could long-term maintenance and sustainable management be assured.

The level of forest expansion assumed in the scenarios for the UNECE region alone are of the same magnitude as the Bonn challenge. This global effort aims to restore 150 million hectares of the world's deforested and degraded land by 2020, and 350 million hectares by 2030. Meeting these goals would secure carbon sequestration similar to the Outlook scenarios. However, five years after adoption of the New York Declaration on Forests (NYDF), there is little evidence that these goals will be achieved (NYDF Assessment Partners, 2019).

### *Potential for carbon storage and substituting carbon intensive materials with wood products and bioenergy*

Strategies to increase wood product use are based on storing carbon in harvested wood products (HWP), and replacing fossil-based or energy-intensive materials like concrete, steel, or glass, as well as substituting wood fibre for fossil-based materials used in plastics and polyester manufacture (Petersen and Solberg 2005; Werner and Richter 2007; Sathre and O'Connor 2010; Leskinen *et al.* 2018; Myllyviita *et al.* 2021)). These strategies could potentially require increased harvesting, with trade-offs in biomass carbon pools, as well as improved recycling rates and extended life for wood products (Brunet-Navarro *et al.*, 2017). There has been progress in estimating the size and changes in the HWP carbon pool but estimating the potential for avoiding carbon emissions by replacing carbon intensive materials with wood is challenging.

The climate benefits of substitution by wood are best estimated by comparing greenhouse gas emissions from the manufacture of a wood product with emissions for manufacturing the product that would be replaced, taking into account its full life from production to end of life (Churkina *et al.*, 2020). Typically, a general substitution or displacement factor is used to quantify greenhouse gas reductions if a wood-based product were used instead of a chemical compound, construction element, energy service, or textile fibre. Estimates of the substitution impact are made by multiplying wood product quantities by the product-specific substitution factor. A literature review of substitution factors found that by far the majority of factors for wood and wood-based products had lower fossil and process-based emissions than equivalent non-wood products (Box 4.2).

This section uses the GFPM scenarios presented in chapter 3 to address the question of system-wide consequences for carbon stocks and flows of increasing the use of wood to substitute for carbon-intensive and non-renewable materials and energy.

### *Substitution in Construction*

Construction (together with related uses such as joinery and furniture) is the major market for sawnwood and panels. Two GFPM scenarios examined the consequences for the sector as a whole of increased use of wood in construction outside the UNECE region (China-HWC) and inside the UNECE region (Europe-HWC). An important element of both scenarios is the likely rise in the use of engineered wood products, such as glulam, cross laminated timber (CLT) and laminated veneer lumber (LVL). The scenarios are described in Chapter 3 and the full paper.

A transition to bio-based building materials will only succeed as a climate mitigation strategy if forests are managed and harvested sustainably to avoid forest degradation and soil depletion. It is also important that wood from existing and future buildings should be recovered and reused, to the extent practicable.

Increasing consumption of forest products outside the UNECE region, based on the assumptions underlying the China-HWC scenario, resulted in higher carbon storage in HWP than in the reference scenario and higher avoided emissions (Table 4.3).

**BOX 4.2**

**Substitution factors**

A review by Leskinen *et al.* (2018) of 51 studies with information on 433 substitution factors suggested an average substitution effect of 2.2 kg $CO_2$ /kg wood, which means that for each kilogram of wood product that substitutes non-wood products, an average emission reduction occurs of approximately 2.2 kg $CO_2$. Substitution factors are highly variable, with 95% of values in the range 1.3-9.3 $CO_2$ /kg wood. This reflects multiple differences between products, the non-wood materials that are substituted, production technologies, numbers of life cycle stages considered, and end-of-life management practice.

The Europe-HWC scenario (which assumed that wood consumption per dwelling in Europe and the Russian Federation would reach the North American average by 2040) projected greater carbon storage in HWP in all UNECE subregions with the exception of the Russian Federation and avoided emissions of 56.8 million $tCO_2e$ per year. The differences between this and the reference scenario are shown in Table 4.4.

**TABLE 4.3 Differences between the China-HWC and reference scenarios, (million $tCO_2e$ per year, annual average 2015-2040)**

| | Biomass | Harvested Wood Products | Avoided emissions in construction | Balance |
|---|---|---|---|---|
| Europe-EU | -10.2 | 2.8 | -1.6 | -9.0 |
| Europe-Other | -1.7 | 0.1 | -0.3 | -1.9 |
| North America | -10.6 | 5.5 | -1.0 | -6.1 |
| EECCA | -0.9 | 1.0 | -0.3 | -0.2 |
| Russian Federation | -7.3 | 2.9 | -0.4 | -4.7 |
| Asia | -204.3 | 73.1 | 143.7 | 12.4 |
| World | -258.6 | 86.7 | 139.7 | -32.2 |
| of which UNECE region | -30.6 | 12.3 | -3.6 | -21.9 |

**Note:** HWP C stocks and flows are assigned to wood producing countries, while avoided emissions are assigned to wood consuming countries.

**Source:** GFPM projections.

**TABLE 4.4 Differences between the Europe-HWC and reference scenarios (million $tCO_2e$ per year, annual average 2015-2040)**

| | Biomass | Harvested Wood Products | Avoided emissions in construction | Balance |
|---|---|---|---|---|
| Europe-EU | -14.4 | 15.6 | 46.5 | 47.7 |
| Europe-Other | -1.7 | 1.2 | 2.7 | 2.2 |
| North America | -11.2 | 4.6 | -0.2 | -6.8 |
| EECCA | -0.8 | 1.5 | 1.8 | 2.5 |
| Russian Federation | -6.1 | -4.0 | 5.9 | -4.2 |
| Asia | -26.7 | 10.5 | -3.4 | -19.6 |
| World | -83.8 | 30.7 | 52.9 | -0.3 |
| of which UNECE region | -34.2 | 18.9 | 56.8 | 41.4 |

**Note:** HWP C stocks and flows are assigned to wood producing countries, while avoided emissions are assigned to wood consuming countries.

**Source:** GFPM projections.

However, as with the China-HWC scenario, the picture is different when changes in forest carbon stock are taken into account. The balance shown in Table 4.4 is positive for the UNECE region, but practically unchanged at the global level.

The values shown are subject to the same uncertainties as the China-HWC scenario.

Both the China-HWC and the Europe-HWC scenario show a positive net carbon effect in the regions where consumption is assumed to increase, but a negative global carbon balance. This highlights the risk of leakage effects between regions.

It should be pointed out that these results are to a certain extent dependent on the time span considered. The balance could be different, perhaps even with a different sign if the time period considered were longer, or shorter.

### *Substitution in Textiles*

Technical and economic developments have made it possible for wood, mostly in the form of chemical pulp, to address the market for feedstock for textiles, at present dominated by hydrocarbons and cotton. A GFPM scenario (Textile-HFWC) (section 3.4.3) examined the consequences for the sector as whole of increased use of wood as feedstock for textiles.

Under this scenario, increased use of wood fibres for textiles avoided global emissions of 77 million $tCO_2e$ per year (Table 4.5).

However, increased competition for wood, leading to higher raw material prices, resulted in increased use of non-wood alternatives (for non-textiles uses) causing emissions from these products to rise by 8.9 million $tCO_2e$ per year. Global forest carbon sequestration in this scenario would be 7%, or 76 million $tCO_2e$ per year lower than in the reference scenario. Only 7% of this projected reduction in global biomass carbon was projected to be offset by global increase in carbon storage in harvested wood products. This was mainly because textiles products are assumed to be short-lived. Furthermore, the biomass sink was significantly lower than in the reference scenario. As a result, at the global level, there was a slight reduction in the forest-related carbon sink. In the UNECE region, the loss of carbon from forest biomass in this scenario was offset, giving an overall small net positive carbon balance.

In addition, it is important to note that the results of the model assume that there is no long-term carbon storage in textiles, as they are not considered a long-lived wood product. In fact, research has shown that lyocell stores more carbon than is emitted during its production (Kalnbalkite *et al.*, 2017). This would be highly relevant if textile products, such as garments

**TABLE 4.5 Differences between the Textile-HWFC and reference scenarios (million $tCO_2e$ per year, annual average, 2015-2040**

| | Biomass | Harvested Wood Products | Avoided emissions | | Balance |
|---|---|---|---|---|---|
| | | | *Textiles* | *Other* | |
| Europe-EU | -7.9 | -1.7 | 11.5 | -1.3 | 0.5 |
| Europe-Other | -1.0 | 0.3 | -0.9 | -0.3 | -1.8 |
| North America | -16.4 | 0.7 | 26.4 | -1.8 | 8.8 |
| EECCA | -0.5 | 0.7 | -0.3 | -0.2 | -0.4 |
| Russian Federation | -3.3 | -2.9 | -0.5 | -0.2 | -6.9 |
| Asia | -18.4 | 7.2 | 27.2 | -4.5 | 11.5 |
| World | -76.1 | 5.4 | 77.0 | -8.9 | -2.6 |
| of which UNECE region | -29.1 | -2.9 | 36.2 | -3.8 | 0.3 |

**Note:** HWP C stocks are assigned to wood producing countries, while avoided emissions are assigned to wood consuming countries. The column "other" refers to emissions occurring in other sectors where wood will be replaced by non-forest materials as a consequence of increased competition for the use of wood.

**Source:** GFPM projections.

had longer lives in use and textile recycling improved, which could significantly extend the life of fibres.

### Substitution in Chemicals

Production processes for chemicals, plastics and composites, which at present are mostly fossil-based, are evolving to use wood-based side streams and coproducts as raw material. This reduces GHG emissions and improves circularity. For example, tall oil or black liquor from pulping is used to generate process energy. Fractionating the crude tall oil into chemical compounds can add significant value to this coproduct. Naphtha is just one derivative used to produce biodiesel or bioplastics (De Bruycker *et al.*, 2014). Some wood-based plastics are already used as linings for beverage cartons. Lignin is another chemical from industrial side streams and could replace fossil-based phenols in several products (Collins *et al.*, 2019). Currently, 50 million tonnes of kraft lignin are produced worldwide annually during pulp production and mostly used for process energy (Lettner *et al.*, 2018). Only 1-2% is recovered and used as raw material for higher-value products, which is a missed opportunity to reduce GHG emissions (Lora and Glasser, 2002).

No scenario was constructed for substitution in the chemical sector, so it is not possible to quantify effects on the global carbon balance of any increase in the use of wood for chemicals.

### Substitution in Energy

In 2010, 35% of global GHG emissions were from the energy sector (IPCC, 2014). By substituting for fossil fuels, wood could potentially decrease the carbon footprint of the energy sector. Changes in demand for wood for energy in the UNECE region are expected to mainly be driven by policy developments.

The most recent UNECE/FAO Joint Wood Energy Enquiry revealed that wood accounts for 35% of all renewable energy in the UNECE region (UNECE/FAO, 2021a). Wood energy generates between two and three times as much as solar, wind, geothermal and hydropower combined. Energy derived from biomass in all its forms accounted for almost 60% of renewable energy in Organization for Economic Co-operation and Development (OECD) countries in 2018, and an even larger share (70%) in non-OECD countries (IEA, 2020).

The primary sources of wood for energy in the UNECE region, are industrial co-products, such as chips, bark, sawdust and shavings from sawmills, as well as material such as black liquor produced from pulping. Together, these account for 51% of wood used for energy. Wood directly harvested from forests, other wooded land, and individual trees accounts for 34%. Post-consumer wood[11] makes up only 5%, and the remaining share cannot be defined (UNECE/FAO, 2021a). These shares remained fairly constant between 2007 and 2017.

The timescales and leakage effects of using wood energy need to be carefully considered to assess whether wood energy can mitigate climate change. Fossil fuels emit less $CO_2$ per unit energy than biomass. In the short-term, therefore, atmospheric $CO_2$ released by burning wood exacerbates climate change (Zanchi *et al.*, 2012). However, the $CO_2$ in wood used for energy was captured from the atmosphere and will be re-captured by forest regrowth under sustainable management. Depending on the biomass feedstock used to generate energy, notably whether it is residues or roundwood and if the latter, its origins (e.g. from thinning or clear-felling), it could take many years, perhaps centuries, to reach parity (Zanchi *et al.*, 2012, Nabuurs *et al.*, 2017). Furthermore, wood residues and post-consumer wood if not used in products, recycled or used for energy, would release carbon as they decompose so there could be an opportunity cost for not using them for energy (unlike wood in the forest which would continue to sequester carbon if not burnt).

11 This includes wood waste from construction, but also packaging and old furniture, and is mainly consumed in power applications and waste-to-energy plants

The carbon footprint of harvesting, processing and transporting wood fuels is lower than for fossil fuels. The revised European Renewable Energy Directive (RED) sets out detailed values for greenhouse gas emissions of biomass fuels and fossil fuel, if produced with no net-carbon emissions from land-use change. For wood energy most pathways indicate a reduction in carbon emissions of 70% to 80%, compared to fossil fuels (European Commission, 2018).

A review of research about wood energy and its impacts on GHG emissions revealed four main insights into its emission-mitigating role (Miner *et al.*, 2014). Though focused primarily on the United States, the conclusions are generally valid.

1) Wood energy reduces fossil fuel use and long-term carbon emissions, provided forest area or growing stock does not decrease.
2) Demand for wood energy provides economic incentives, such as higher timber prices, encouraging investment in forestry, increasing forest area and productivity, helping offset emissions from additional harvesting and wood burning.
3) Though burning wood can increase short-term emissions, long-term cumulative biogenic $CO_2$ emissions are reduced by replacing fossil fuel.
4) Over 100 years, increased use of wood energy in the United States would result in lower net GHG emissions, compared with fossil fuel emissions.

Energy and climate policies are designed to cut energy and transport sector emissions, increase energy efficiency and raise the share of energy from renewable sources. The Renewable Energy Directives (RED) I and II of the European Union set the most ambitious goals for renewable energy in the UNECE region. Given that wood energy already accounts for a significant share of renewable energy, these regulations are likely to strongly impact wood use by the energy sector. In mid-2021, there is a vigorous discussion, which has not yet been resolved, over the role of wood energy in the future renewable energy supply of the EU.

The second European Forest Sector Outlook Study modelled the impact of promoting wood energy in Europe, based on the RED I goals (UNECE/FAO, 2011). It concluded that it would be technically possible for wood to supply 40% of renewable energy, as foreseen by the Directive, but only if energy efficiency improved and all potential biomass sources were mobilized. This would include harvesting as much as possible of the annual volume increment, sevenfold increase in extraction of harvesting residues, doubling the volume of landscape care wood and post-consumer wood, and tripling imports. Achieving such a large increase in wood supplies would entail significant trade-offs, especially for land use and biodiversity. Many other factors would present a challenge, including increasing the workforce and harvest equipment pool to achieve such levels. It remains questionable whether this would be achievable (Orazio *et al.*, 2017).

A study looked at how a doubling of wood consumption by the United States wood energy sector between 2015 and 2050 might affect the net carbon status of the United States forest products sector, compared to a base scenario (Nepal *et al.*, 2019c). It found that higher consumption of wood energy would lead to higher timber prices. Since United States timberland area tends to respond positively to timber prices, the study projected that the timberland area in this high wood energy scenario would be 2.5%, or 5.2 million hectares, higher than projected for the base assumption, and that timber stocks would also be higher. The projected increase in forest stocks suggests there would be a net increase in carbon sequestration from expanded wood energy use.

## 4.4 Climate change adaptation

**KEY QUESTION:**

***How can UNECE forests adapt to climate change?***

Forest management has evolved over centuries to meet demand for forest products and ecosystem services under climate conditions which appeared stable and predictable or at worst subject to gradual change. However, as evidence mounts that the climate is changing now, and will change more in the future, forest managers must reflect on how to adapt to this radically new situation (Box 4.3).

This section describes potential forest management strategies and adaptation measures, at the stand, local and national levels to respond to this uncertain future.

### *4.4.1 Adaptation in natural and managed forests*

Adaptation may occur through natural processes, such as genetic selection, or through management. The inherent adaptive capacity of forests allows them to be resilient in the face of changing environmental conditions over longer time frames. Yet, genetic adaptive processes are still poorly understood, and their potential role in adapting forests to rapid anthropogenic climate change is even less well understood (Lindner *et al.*, 2010). Some management strategies designed to facilitate forest adaptation are founded on the principles of adaptive forest management. They utilize ecological understanding of future climate change impacts to create a resilient forest that is able to cope with a range of future conditions while still providing the main services requested by society, and are adapted as necessary in the light of the evolving situation. Interventions such as planting better-adapted species, tending and thinning, are intended to enhance forest adaptive capacity by adjusting structure and composition. Such adaptation measures depend on data

availability and projections that assess how forests might react to future climate change. Developing adaptation strategies will also depend on funding and other socioeconomic factors, including availability of a skilled workforce.

### 4.4.2 *Adaptive forest management*

Adaptation measures may be reactive or proactive. Reactive measures respond to climate change following an impact such as a disturbance or die-back, for example by planting alternative tree species. Waiting until the impact of climate change becomes evident, and only then taking targeted management action, involves a high degree of risk. This approach could result in the loss of ecosystem services, such as a diminution of scenic landscape value with consequences for tourism, or losses in protective services. Delaying action could result in higher volumes of dead or damaged timber, due to disturbances, magnifying economic effects on landowners and timber processors.

**BOX 4.3**

**How quickly could forest management adapt?**

Forests management cycles range from decades for fast-growing, intensively-managed plantations, to centuries for slow-growing managed forests. The timeframe for adapting forests will depend on initial condition, predicted changes in climate, management system employed, as well as the willingness of owners to actively manage change. Financial and scientific support will also play a strong role. Generally, disturbed, harvested and young stands offer the greatest opportunities to swiftly enhance adaptive capacity by altering forest structure and species composition, through planting, natural regeneration, tending and thinning. Later growth stages are more difficult because stem numbers have often already been reduced but these stands (assuming they are even-aged) are also closer to being harvested and replaced anyway. Forest management will need to adapt continuously as environmental conditions and society's expectations change. For example, vulnerable spruce stands in Central Europe are being underplanted with beech and fir 30 years before final harvest, so that they integrate into the stand through continuous cover management. Recent years have seen dieback of beech and fir following successive summer droughts. It remains unclear how beech and fir species will recover and whether young stands will adapt better than mature ones. Monitoring how forests respond to site factors, climate and its associated extremes and disturbances, and earlier management regimes, will become essential to allow early introduction of measures which provide fast and suitable adjustments to forest management strategies. The speed of adaptation will require integration of natural and human-driven adaptive strategies. Examples include encouraging genetic diversity, and using silviculture to introduce new provenances of existing species (e.g. planting seedlings from the same species growing in a hotter and drier climate), or mixtures of species.

Proactive management on the other hand takes place before climate change-induced impacts have occurred, with the aim of preventing or alleviating expected negative impacts. It could mean adopting mixtures of species, or reducing stand density to diminish the likelihood of disturbance and damage. Proactive management also carries risk, arising from the necessity of taking silvicultural actions before their long-term consequences can be properly researched. Examples of possible negative consequences of proactive silvicultural measures are introducing less well-adapted species or genotypes, disturbing stand stability during thinning, and creating openings that might allow the introduction of invasive exotic plants.

Whether reactive or proactive measures are adopted, the scale and timing of specific adaptation measures will depend on local circumstances. A list of possible reactive and proactive adaptations to deal with current and future bark beetle impacts appears below (Table 4.6).

The objective of most proactive adaptation measures is to spread risks among stand members. A conversion of monocultures into mixed forests can for example alleviate disturbance impacts and simultaneously boost forest productivity (Pretzsch *et al.*, 2013). Likewise, increasing genetic and structural diversity leads to higher resource use efficiency (Pretzsch *et al.*, 2016, Zeller *et al.*, 2018, Liang *et al.*, 2016) and resilience against disturbance impacts (Jactel *et al.*, 2017, Sousa-Silva 2018).

Other measures concern management techniques. A reduction of rotation length can very effectively decrease a forest's vulnerability to disturbance (Seidl, 2011). Tending and thinning, on the other hand, promote individual tree performance. With the initial aim to direct growth towards individual trees with the highest expected

**TABLE 4.6 Examples of short-term, medium term and long-term reactive and proactive adaptation options to deal with bark beetle impacts on forests at stand, landscape and policy levels**

| | ***Short-term (< 5 years)*** | |
|---|---|---|
| | ***Reactive*** | ***Proactive*** |
| Stand | Restore economic value, e.g. by salvage logging | Reduce competition, e.g. tending, thinning to increase vitality of remaining trees |
| Landscape | Spatial and temporal planning of post disturbance management to facilitate joint action (e.g. organisation of salvage logging across different ownerships) | Monitor severity and movement of bark beetle infestation and prevent spread of bark beetles, e.g. by sanitary fellings |
| Policy/ governance | Promote pest and disturbance management, e.g. tax reductions for salvaged timber | Promote access to forests and adaptive forest management, e.g. subsidies for road building, storage places for salvage logged timber |
| | ***Medium-term (5-10 years)*** | |
| | ***Reactive*** | ***Proactive*** |
| Stand | Intensified management, e.g. increased thinning regimes to reduce risk | Promoting mixing of species to reduce the number of susceptible trees, e.g. by fostering in growing trees from other species than the main species |
| Landscape | Knowledge gain, e.g. monitoring programs to monitor severity and movement of bark beetle infestation | Adaptation experience, e.g. exchange among forest managers |
| Policy/ governance | Incentivize management actions about how to deal with bark beetle damage, e.g. education campaigns how to clean affected stands | Seed transfers, e.g. relax national trading restrictions |
| | ***Long-term (> 10 years)*** | |
| | ***Reactive*** | ***Proactive*** |
| Stand | Intensified management, e.g. plantation economy with short rotations | Forest conversion towards uneven-aged, mixed species to spread infestation risk |
| Landscape | Development of infrastructure to shorten reaction times to contain bark beetle spread: e.g. road building, storage places of salvage logged timber | Temporal and spatial planning of management actions to increase landscape heterogeneity |
| Policy/ governance | Funding programmes to improve disaster risk management, e.g. by funding infrastructure as described above | Funding programmes to enhance resilience, e.g. forest type conversion |

**Source:** Authors' own work.

timber value, resistance to disturbance also increases after a short-time drop (Sohn *et al.*, 2016).

### 4.4.3 Adaptation at the stand level

#### Forest regeneration

Regeneration offers an opportunity to lay the foundation for adaptation. Ideally, the next generation of trees will have potential to deal with future climatic conditions. There is a presumption that if the parent trees performed well, their progeny would perform similarly, although this assumption may not hold under a changed climate regime. Natural regeneration may be considered in management plans as an option for forest regeneration. If the natural regeneration fails to appear, is expected to occur in undesired states, or cannot survive future disturbance regimes, planting may compensate. Enrichment plantings can supplement natural regeneration or substitute for it. Sometimes planting or seeding non-native tree species or different origins/provenances may benefit adaptive capacity. Choosing the species, origin/provenance, mixed planting, densities, and planting methods, should be based on available information from field experiments, observations and modelling, even if incomplete, to minimise maladaptation or failure.

#### Tending and thinning

Tending and thinning remove individual trees, reduce stand densities and modify species compositions. After a short drop in productivity, the remaining trees compensate for the removal (Dieler *et al.*, 2017). Trees in thinned stands are better able to withstand drought stress and maintain defences against pests and diseases (Sohn *et al.*, 2016; Bottero *et al.*, 2017). Opening the canopy by thinning may increase short-term susceptibility to storm damage, but once crowns have reconnected, the stand will be more storm-resistant, with better crown depth, improved height-diameter stem ratio, and root growth (Slodicak & Novak, 2006). The additional growing space gives the tree better access to soil nutrients and soil water, reducing the effects of heat and drought (Sohn *et al.*, 2012).

#### Forest type conversion

Forest conversion gradually transforms the species composition and structure of forest stands poorly adapted to the changing climatic conditions so they have better adaptive potential, while minimizing any reduction in provisioning services. At present, the most common conversions change single-species forests into mixed-species forests, and even-aged forests into uneven-aged forests. Techniques include establishing shade-tolerant species under a mature stand before final harvest, by natural regeneration or planting. Low intensity thinning slowly increases light at the forest floor, allowing establishment of more light-demanding species. The process requires time to secure a balanced mix between shade-tolerant and light-demanding species. Achieving an uneven-aged structure requires even more time. Conversions may take up to 80 years and require low intensity management intervention at various times, and at differing scales.

#### Post-disturbance management

Post-disturbance management may include salvage logging after storm or fire damage, sanitation felling following disease or pest outbreaks, and planting to replace losses. Salvage logging is the most common response, with the aim of cutting economic losses, reducing hazardous conditions, and preventing subsequent problems, like bark beetle outbreaks after a storm. Salvage logging reduces forest carbon stock through removal of dead or damaged trees, but lets living trees continue to sequester carbon (Molinas-Gonzáles *et al.*, 2017). Recently, possible adverse effects of salvage logging on the recovery of biodiversity and ecosystem resilience have been identified (Leverkus *et al.*, 2018). Large, unplanned volumes of salvage stock can cause roundwood prices to drop, and the fall may be enough to make salvage operations uneconomic. Where salvage is not expected to reduce damage from subsequent disturbances, alternative approaches, such as non-intervention, may be considered (Dobor *et al.*, 2019). By removing dead or weakened trees, sanitary felling contains further spread of insects or pathogens. Disturbances arising because of climate change, may even provide an opportunity to plant better-adapted species mixtures. However, sometimes non-intervention may be a preferred option, promoting natural regeneration and thereby encouraging a more diverse and species-rich forests structure. This in turn may help build heightened resilience to future disturbances (Seidl. *et al.*, 2016).

### 4.4.4 Adaptation beyond the stand level

Forest governance has always been complex, but has become more so in the past three decades, with multiple layers of authority, increasing stakeholder interest, and sometimes conflicting policies impinging on forest management. Responsibility for policies affecting forest management are shared between local, state, and national bodies in all UNECE member States, which may limit options for defining and achieving goals at the regional level.

However, the current system also offers potential to produce flexible and adaptive responses to local circumstances. Adaptation policies and measures can be designed to empower local, regional or national government and agencies to take account of local circumstances and forest priorities. Responding to disturbances will often require urgent measures to mitigate economic impacts, and local bodies are often best equipped to respond quickly, even if they may require supplementary financial and technical resources to face the emerging challenges. Where there is a need for a coordinated, cross-sectoral approach, this may be best led at the national level, guided by national and international policies. Measures available at regional or national government level could include long-term arrangements between forest owners and processing industries, tax reductions for salvaged timber, financial assistance for sanitary felling, adaptive management, and temporary easing of legal constraints.

Effective adaptation requires policies and measures that cover the immediate response, and more long-term proactive/preparatory action. These will differ with location and state of management (Nabuurs *et al.*, 2019). For instance, in an intensively-managed area, policies promoting a resilient forest sector which can secure long-term raw material supplies may take precedence. In areas that experience hotspots of disturbance, actions that focus on the transition to a long-term resilient forest ecosystem may take priority. Economic and ecological disturbance impacts could be reduced if countries establish a regulatory and managerial environment supporting rapid response at local and regional levels, with national leadership that encourages cross-sectoral cooperation.

### 4.4.5 *National adaptation strategies*

Most UNECE member States are signatories to international agreements on forests, recognizing the challenges of climate change, deforestation and forest degradation. The United Nations Strategic Plan for Forests 2017-2030, aims to prevent and reverse forest cover loss and forest degradation through sustainable forest management, protection, restoration, reforestation, and afforestation. Measures to improve forests' adaptive capacity and resilience to meet predicted climate change are explicitly listed in the Strategic Plan. The Global Forest Goals refer to climate change mitigation and adaptation (United Nations, 2017). How to achieve these goals is decided by national governments, resulting in widely-varied adaptation strategies.

Most UNECE countries have national cross-sectoral strategic plans for adaptation to climate change, though forests may not be mentioned except in reference to other sectors. Detailed descriptions and assessments of national adaptation strategies have been published for pan-Europe (Forest Europe, 2020); the Russian Federation (Leskinen *et al.*, 2020); and Canada (Environment and Climate Change Canada, 2016).

In the United States, the USDA Forest Service has worked with other federal agencies on adaptation measures in national forests and national grasslands. State governments and some Native American tribes and communities have taken formal steps to adapt forests to climate change (Vose *et al.*, 2018). However, there is no overall federal policy to guide land managers in what approach to take in adapting forest management to climate change (Keskitalo and Preston, 2019).

The European Union has made several forest-related climate commitments. In particular, The European Green Deal contains a commitment to improve the EU forest area, in quantity and quality, for the EU to reach climate neutrality and a healthy environment[12] (European Commission, 2019). A revised EU forest strategy is being prepared. In the Russian Federation, national forestry authorities included climate change in forestry planning in 2017 and added the requirement to develop adaptation measures in forest plans (Leskinen *et al.*, 2020). Examples of three adaptation approaches at the national level in Europe are shown in Box 4.4.

**BOX 4.4**

**Examples of national forest adaptation strategies across Europe**

A recent report summarizes the state of forest adaptation in Europe (Forest Europe, 2020). Three examples from the report for Eastern Europe (Czech Republic), central-European mountain regions (Switzerland) and the Mediterranean region (Spain) are described next, including material from additional sources.

Forests in the **Czech Republic** have suffered from a series of storms, severe droughts, and bark beetle infestations, which damaged almost 100 million $m^3$ between 2010 and 2020, with severe effects on timber markets (Toth *et al.*, 2020). the Czech Republic adopted a cross-sectoral adaptation strategy in 2015, looking ahead to 2030. Though not explicitly enforced by legislation, forest adaptation is a major element of the national forest programme. Propelled by incentives and tax relief, forest management strategies, such as close-to-nature forestry and intensified management, are encouraged, with emphases on changing tree species and improving forest water retention capacity. Changes to tree species composition have had government and legislative support since 1996. The Czech Republic actively supports planting species which improve soil condition and stabilize forests, reforestation, stand establishment and follow-up management. Recently, support has been extended to cover reactive measures following disturbances. Since 2000, stand inventories have shown more than a 5% reduction overall in vulnerable conifer species, and more than 15% in stands aged 1–20 years, suggesting that these measures have been effective.

In 2006, **Spain** implemented a cross-sectoral climate change adaptation strategy, introducing action plans for forest adaptation. Financial support has been provided for close-to-nature and intensified management measures; use of good quality genetic stock for replanting and afforestation; improvements to promote water retention; and agroforestry. Spain recorded the worst wildfires in Europe from 2010 to 2020, affecting more than 100,000 ha/

12 In addition, it states that « sustainable re- and afforestation and the restoration of degraded forests can increase absorption of $CO_2$ while improving the resilience of forests and promoting the circular bio-economy".

year, and has launched fire prevention measures, including constructing firebreaks; removal cuttings; pruning; prescribed burning; forest debris removal; and planting fire-resistant species and reducing arson. During the winter of 2018, in a programme of controlled burning coordinated by the Integral Prevention teams (EPRIF) in collaboration with farmers, 526 ha of forest were treated with 100 prescribed and controlled fires. Another collaboration between the Preventive Work Brigades from the Ministry of Agriculture and the autonomous administrations, applied preventive silvicultural measures on over 1300 hectares. Measures included thinning, pruning, and underbrush removal, carried out in 11 months by more than 400 workers.

**Switzerland** adopted its adaptation strategy in 2012. It includes a 2020–2025 Action Plan supported by federal legislation, as well as financial and institutional support. Close-to-nature forestry is practiced in almost all forests. Switzerland uses a combination of advanced technologies to guide forest adaption, among which is an automated warning system to map forest fire risk at local, regional and federal levels. To guide climate-change-oriented decision-making, the national research programme, "Forests and Climate Change" supported development of the "Tree-App". which projects future development of Swiss forests and provides users with a system to select tree species ecologically suited to local circumstances. In 2018, the Federal Office for the Environment (FOEN) and the Swiss Federal Institute for Forest and Landscape Research (WSL), launched a project to investigate how tree species suited to Switzerland might perform during climate change. The trial tested seven provenances of 18 species across 57 regionally-distributed sites. The Swiss adaptation strategy also acknowledges the role of "urban-forestry" in reducing heat stress and preventing heat-islands in cities, improving health-enhancing effects and benefiting biodiversity.

## 4.5 Overview: balancing impacts, mitigation, and adaptation

This section examines the balance and interaction between climate change impacts, and mitigation and adaptation measures.

Forests across the UNECE region are likely to be impacted by changes in average growing conditions and extreme events, brought about by climate change. The effects of climate change on the processes that underpin forest growth and productivity are complex and uncertain. An extended growing season, warmer temperatures and higher atmospheric $CO_2$ levels might increase productivity in some countries and regions, but might also be accompanied by increased risk of drought and disruption from fire, disease, and insect outbreaks. These changes may have a more profound effect on productivity than assumed in current models.

Changes in productivity and species distribution will be highly variable, and may affect forest product markets, giving rise to changes in the comparative advantages between regions. Underlying uncertainty about forest growth changes and market implications mean that modelling results need to be viewed with a degree of caution. For instance, if projected growth increases did not arise because actual physiological adaption to higher levels of $CO_2$ differs from assumptions built into the vegetation models underlying these projections, the projected changes in forest product prices might well not occur.

Natural disturbances, which are becoming more frequent because of climate change, are a challenge for forest management and wood processing. Salvage logging and sanitary cutting produce unexpected and temporary workloads. This may drive down timber prices, disrupting management plans and operations like harvesting and regeneration. Delaying thinning or final felling could affect

**TABLE 4.7 Current and future carbon stocks and fluxes in the reference scenario and different mitigation options of the UNECE region**

| | | Overview reference scenario | | | | | Mitigation | |
|---|---|---|---|---|---|---|---|---|
| | Fossil fuel emissions (as flux) 2018*** | Biomass stock 2015 | Biomass flux 2015-2040 | Harvested Wood Products stock 2015 | Harvested Wood Products flux 2015-2040 | Disturbance flux | Forest management | Afforestation |
| | *$tCO_2e$ per year* | *$tCO_2e$* | *$tCO_2e$ per year* | *$tCO_2e$* | *$tCO_2e$ per year* | *$tCO_2e$ per year* | *$tCO_2e$ per year* | *$tCO_2e$ per year* |
| | | | | | *billions* | | | |
| Europe-EU | -3.2 | 35.5 | 0.5 | 5.1 | 0.1 | -0.2* | 0-0.21 | 0.2 |
| Europe-Other | -0.5 | 7.5 | 0.1 | 0.5 | 0.0 | -0.2* | 0-0.04 | 0.05 |
| North America | -5.9 | 130.1 | 0.7 | 5.9 | 0.0 | -0.7** | 0-0.5 | 0.6 |
| EECCA | -0.7 | 8.4 | 0.1 | 0.4 | 0.0 | na | na | 0.05 |
| Russian Federation | -1.6 | 121.4 | 0.1 | 2.4 | 0.0 | -0.3 | na | 0.5 |
| UNECE region | -11.9 | 302.9 | 1.5 | 14.3 | 0.2 | -1.2 | 0.8 | 1.4 |
| Rest of the world | -21.6 | 1046.7 | -0.3 | 10.0 | 0.3 | na | 0-1.3 | 4.4 |
| World | -33.5 | 1349.6 | 1.2 | 24.3 | 0.5 | na | 0.4-2.1 | 5.9 |

**Notes:** Stocks and flux for biomass and harvested wood products (HWP) are based on the modelling with GFPM in this Outlook, effects of disturbance (section 4.2.3), forest management and afforestation (section 4.3.2) are based on the literature review presented in this Outlook and GFPM results. For fluxes, a negative sign indicates a source, positive signs a sink. *for 2021-2030 from Seidl *et al.*, 2014. ** for recent period. *** Source: energyatlas.iea.org

stand stability, generating a negative loop that makes forests susceptible to subsequent disturbance. Over the longer term, this could threaten ecosystem services. The models used in this study do not typically include an in-depth analysis of such effects on forest products markets and forest productivity. This leaves questions, such as "will more frequent extreme events, like heat waves and persistent drought, cancel out climate-induced productivity gains?", or "what are the exact implications for the global timber market of frequent, large-scale disturbances?"

Forests play an important role in mitigating climate change. The mitigation effect is influenced by the carbon stored in biomass, litter, soil, deadwood and wood products, and changes brought about by climate change, plus the contribution of avoided emissions, when wood products substitute carbon-intensive products and fossil energy (Table 4.7).

The carbon stock in forest biomass is large, and the forest sink (the annual net absorption of $CO_2$ by forests) is only a fraction of that. The average annual projected increase in forest biomass carbon storage (net carbon sink expressed as % of the biomass stock) in this Outlook was 0.5% in North America, 1.3% in Europe-EU, 1.8% in Europe-Other, 1.7% in EECCA, and 0.1% in the Russian Federation totaling 0.5% in the UNECE region as a whole from 2015 until 2040. In 2015, harvested wood products (HWP) stored a small fraction of carbon: 5% of forest biomass stock in the UNECE region as a whole, but 15% in Europe, which is a main producer of HWP.

Based on a literature review, the current disturbance effects on carbon may be as large as the net carbon sink of forests in the UNECE region (Table 4.7). Although forest management measures may increase the forest carbon sink by 50-100%, research suggests that increased disturbance frequency and intensity may offset all or part of these additional carbon gains. Forest management strategies for climate change mitigation must account for forest disturbances, and adaptation and mitigation measures should be considered together (Box 4.5).

Increasing global forest area by 10% by 2040 would sequester 2.94 billion $tCO_2e$ per year in the UNECE region as opposed to the 1.5 billion $tCO_2e$ per year of the baseline scenario, resulting in additional 1.43 billion $tCO_2e$ per year during 2015-2040.

Scenarios aimed at increased production of wood to substitute fossil-based alternatives were projected to be nearly carbon neutral, both for textiles and wood construction until 2040. Longer time-horizons could produce different results. There is considerable variation, especially around the substitution factors. The greatest changes in net carbon emissions would be obtained by substituting the most fossil energy-intensive non-wood materials by wood and wood fibres. Furthermore, these scenarios show effects in other regions, as wood is partly produced outside of the region where it is consumed and reductions in wood supply in one region may be counterbalanced by increases elsewhere. The effect of the substitution option can be further increased by improving wood product production efficiency and by minimising forest and production losses. Overall, large uncertainties still revolve around the quantification of carbon storage in HWP and its substitution effects. Results depend very much on the approach and data used (e.g. Box 4.2) but, in summary, this assessment finds that material substitution can have a positive net contribution to climate change mitigation but that positive substitution effects only occur if all the interlinked aspects are properly addressed, in a holistic fashion.

Forests and forest management will need to adapt to a changing climate to maintain their multiple functions. Adaptation may happen naturally, or by adapting forest management. Changing management will require a qualified workforce and might require investment in monitoring, research and forest management. Climate change not only makes adaptation necessary, but might also provide an opportunity to put adaptation measures into practice. Disturbances may make it possible for silvicultural measures to adjust species composition to be effective in a shorter time frame.

Ideally adaptation and mitigation would be considered together, when anticipating how best to combine measures to react to changing environmental and socio-economic conditions. Trade-offs between sometimes competing management objectives, as well as mitigation and adaptation options, need to be considered within the context of changing demands on the forest and make explicit the trade-offs and synergies between nature conservation, forest carbon sequestration, forest product carbon sequestration and substituting carbon intensive products with low carbon forest products. Large-scale, disruptive disturbances might influence societal discourse about adaptation options and mitigation potential. These ideas are brought together in the concept of Climate-Smart Forestry which is described in Box 4.5.

**BOX 4.5**

**Climate-Smart Forestry**

Mitigation and adaptation are rarely considered together when considering national strategies to implement climate action. Climate-Smart Forestry (CSF) is a holistic approach that connects mitigation with adaptation measures, guiding forest management in Europe to enhance the resilience of forest resources and ecosystem services, and meet the needs of a growing population (Nabuurs *et al.*, 2017; Jandl *et al.*, 2018; Yousefpour *et al.*, 2018; Bowditch *et al.*, 2020, Verkerk *et al.*, 2020). CSF builds on the concepts of sustainable forest management, with a strong focus on climate and ecosystem services. It uses three mutually-reinforcing components:

- Increasing carbon storage in forests and wood products, in conjunction with provisioning of other ecosystem services.
- Enhancing forest health and resilience through adaptive management.
- Using wood resources sustainably to substitute non-renewable, carbon-intensive materials.

CSF aims at a mix of these by developing spatially diverse forest management strategies that acknowledge all carbon pools, emissions and removals simultaneously to provide longer-term and larger mitigation benefits, while supporting biodiversity and other ecosystem services. Such strategies should combine measures to maintain or increase carbon stocks in forest ecosystems and wood products, and maximize substitution benefits, while taking regional conditions into account (Nabuurs *et al.*, 2017; Verkerk *et al.*, 2020).

# 5 Cross cutting issues

## Key points

- Forest and forest management are linked to a variety of SDGs. The strongest links are to SDG12 (sustainable production and consumption), SDG13 (climate action), and SDG15 (life on land).

- The scenarios analysed will affect biodiversity, for instance through increased forest area, increased wood harvest, and changes in species distribution ranges and disturbance.

- The nature of forest jobs is changing as more of workers find employment outside the classical forestry sector, in areas such as social and urban development, biodiversity and ecosystem functioning, or health and recreation.

- There is a will to attract more women to forestry jobs and to achieve a better gender balance. International forest certification schemes include gender-relevant questions among their requirements.

- Only hypothetical assumptions can be made on the long-term effect of pandemics on the forest sector.

## 5.1 Introduction

This study focused on the six priority questions identified at the beginning of the FSOS process, grouped around structural changes in the forest sector and climate change, and analysed in chapters 3 and 4. However, there are several major cross-cutting issues which are important for the outlook, but could not be analysed in the same depth. This short chapter reviews the possible outlook for the major issues of forest biodiversity, workforce, and the role of women in the forest sector, and analyses the potential impact on these issues of the scenarios presented in this study. In addition, the scenarios will be put into the context of the UN's Sustainable Development Goals (SDGs).

The COVID-19 pandemic, which started when this study was nearly complete, could not be taken into account in the in-depth analysis. However, short term effects on the forest sector are already visible, and possible long-term consequences should be examined. This chapter reviews some of the interactions between the pandemic and the forest sector, as a starting point for future analysis.

## 5.2 FSOS and the SDGs

The UN Sustainable Development Agenda 2030, agreed by world leaders in 2015, established 17 Sustainable Development Goals (SDGs) to be achieved by 2030. FAO's "State of the World's Forests 2018" (FAO, 2018) confirms that forests and trees, when managed sustainably, provide a wide range of beneficial products and services and thereby contribute to meeting the 17 SDGs. In particular, forests are a source of food, medicine and fuel for more than a billion people. They help to respond to climate change, protect soils and water, support significant biodiversity and provide many products and services that contribute to socioeconomic development. This is particularly important to hundreds of millions of people in rural areas, including many of the world's poorest (FAO, 2018).

Forests and their sustainable management have significant positive impacts on 28 specific targets in a subset of the SDGs. The most direct links are with SDG 6 (clean water), SDG 13 (climate action) and SDG 15 (life on land). There are also important connections between forests and SDG 1 (no poverty), SDG 2 (zero hunger), SDG 5 (gender equality), SDG 7 (affordable and clean energy), SDG 8 (decent work and economic growth), SDG 11 (sustainable cities and communities) and SDG 12 (sustainable consumption and production) (FAO, 2018).

The analysis of this study addresses a number of issues relevant to the achievement of the SDGs, in particular the achievement of sustainable forest management (target 15.2), sustainable consumption patterns for forest products (target 12.2) and the forest sector's contribution to climate change mitigation, including substitution, and adaptation (target 13.1). Table 5.1 provides cross references between FSOS analysis and the SDG targets which are most relevant to the forest sector.

**TABLE 5.1 Cross references between FSOS analysis and relevant SDG targets**

| FSOS analysis | SDG target |
|---|---|
| FSOS as a whole (sustainability of forest management, globally, and in the UNECE region). | **15.2** By 2020, promote the implementation of sustainable management of all types of forests, halt deforestation, restore degraded forests and substantially increase afforestation and reforestation globally |
| Scenarios on structural changes in demand (3.4) and carbon storage and substituting carbon intensive materials with wood products and bioenergy (4.3.2.3). | **12.2** By 2030, achieve the sustainable management and efficient use of natural resources |
| Analysis of forest sector contribution to climate change mitigation, and adaptation (Chapter 4) | **13.1** Strengthen resilience and adaptive capacity to climate-related hazards and natural disasters in all countries |

SUSTAINABLE DEVELOPMENT GOALS

FAO (2018) concluded that "forests and trees reach out across the SDGs". The same is true for the scenarios presented in this outlook covering issues across a variety of SDGs.

## 5.3 Biodiversity

Forests are diverse ecosystems that are home to a significant part of terrestrial biodiversity. High levels of biodiversity – at the genetic, species and ecosystem levels - are essential for forest ecosystems to remain resilient to environmental changes, including those related to climate change (Mori, Lertzman and Gustafsson, 2017; Malhi *et al.*, 2020). Forests made up of multiple tree species use resources more efficiently, usually store more carbon and are more resistant to pests and diseases than trees in species-poor forests (Jactel *et al.*, 2017). The concept of multifunctionality of forests implies that all these functions and benefits can be delivered simultaneously, yet trade-offs exist between biodiversity conservation, forest management for mitigation and adaptation and other management objectives.

Forests in the UNECE region are experiencing increasing pressures from climate change, which is a significant threat to biodiversity. Warmer, drier growing conditions and increased frequency and severity of natural disturbances have direct and indirect effects on forest biodiversity (for more information, see section 4.2). The impacts of climate change on biodiversity are already observed in the UNECE region as changes in species composition and ranges, shifts in length of growing seasons and changes in the way species interact (Bytnerowicz, Omasa and Paoletti, 2007; Klein Goldewijk, 2017). Forest species become more vulnerable to new pests, diseases and invasive species (Potter and Urquhart 2017; Venälainen *et al.*, 2020). The effects vary widely by region (Gazol *et al.*, 2017). The loss of biodiversity impacts ecosystem functioning, as well as resilience to disturbances and to climate change. Furthermore, climate change reinforces other human-driven factors such as changes in land use and invasive species, leading to cumulative pressures on biodiversity. Climate change mitigation and adaptation strategies can affect biodiversity and ecosystem services both positively and negatively. Land-use conversion, such as afforestation and reforestation, may impact biodiversity negatively or positively, which again may alter the levels of greenhouse gas emissions, thus affecting the global climate (Smith *et al.*, 2018; Freer-Smith *et al.*, 2019; Doelman *et al.*, 2020).

Climate change impacts, and the loss of biodiversity are both projected to worsen in the future. The CBD, IPCC and IPBES have on their agendas the cross-cutting issue of biodiversity and climate change and call for solutions to tackle the effects of climate change, biodiversity loss, desertification, forest degradation and conversion.

The European Forest Sector Outlook Study II (EFSOS II) analysed the potential effects of implementing policies which give priority to biodiversity in forest management. The EFSOS II scenario implements this by assuming, for example, longer rotation periods, forest species conversion after clear cutting, no residue extraction, and more forest area designated for biodiversity conversion. The results indicate that win-win situations in terms of carbon stock, forest growth, and biodiversity conservation are possible. However, these elements need to be balanced with economic interests to ensure adequate wood supply (UNECE/FAO, 2011).

It is possible to identify some biodiversity-related interactions with the scenarios explored in this study. The consequences for biodiversity of certain aspects considered in this FSOS could be as follows:

- **Increased forest area** for mitigation of climate change, would have as its priority objective carbon sequestration, requiring in all likelihood rather intensive forest management (section 3.5.1). Biodiversity in these new forests might be less than in more traditional forests – although possibly biologically richer than the previous land use, which was probably agriculture. Each case would be different: mixed, biodiverse forestry replacing intensive agriculture might be positive for biodiversity, while intensive silviculture on extensively cultivated, biodiverse former agricultural land might be negative.
- **Increased wood harvests**, to satisfy higher demand, or to substitute fossil intensive materials or fuels (sections 3.5 and 4.3.2): the main influence on biodiversity would be in the silvicultural choices for replacing the harvested forest[13], and in the biodiversity characteristics of the harvested forests. If the management objective at the regeneration phase were to maximise wood production and the silvicultural choice is intensive monoculture, the consequences for biodiversity could be negative. If regeneration focused on maintaining or improving biodiversity, for instance with mixed species, the consequences would be positive.
- As climate changes, **species distribution ranges** and the associated forest types are changing (section 4.2.2). There is concern that the migration speed of many tree species may not be able to keep up with the changing climatic conditions and that the receding edges of species distribution ranges are often characterised by strong susceptibility to disturbances like drought, pathogens and insects. In this period of species change, the nature of biodiversity in the affected forests will change, but it is not yet clear in what way, to what extent or at what speed.
- Increasing **disturbances**, due to climate change, will impact biodiversity (section 4.2.3). Disturbances will harm some existing biodiversity and favour other species by changing natural succession and changing biodiversity within affected forests. Furthermore, if the disturbance destroys a stand, the silvicultural choices after the disturbance, (e.g. choosing mixed species, mixed age stands, longer rotations), will affect biodiversity.

The outlook for biodiversity will be determined by the forest strategies chosen, which should seek to provide the optimum combination of wood production, carbon sequestration and storage, biodiversity conservation and the other forest functions. For instance, Climate Smart Forestry (see Box 4.5) aims to develop spatially-diverse forest management strategies that take account of all carbon pools, emissions and removals

13 This assumes there is not continuous cover forestry.

to provide longer-term and larger mitigation benefits, while supporting biodiversity and other ecosystem services.

In addition, there are high level political commitments to conserve biodiversity, notably the Aichi targets. It may therefore be safely assumed that, in line with these commitments, the area of forest protected for biodiversity will not be reduced. In fact, the FAO's Global Forest Resources Assessment 2020 (FAO, 2020) has shown that most of the world is well on track to achieving Aichi Target 11 - 17% of land legally protected for the conservation of biodiversity – with regard to forests, although protected areas represent only one facet of what is needed to conserve biodiversity. The situation is however not good for the other Aichi targets: the IPBES recently stated that "it is likely that most of the Aichi Biodiversity Targets for 2020 will be missed" (IPBES 2019)

## 5.4 Forest workforce

Over the past half century, the forest sector has undergone significant structural and organizational changes, from large corporate structures to sector fragmentation and the outsourcing of work to contractors and seasonal workers. In addition, the rise of ecological awareness and increasing competition between different forest functions has influenced forest management objectives. They have evolved from a focus on extraction of natural resources to including aspects such as conservation and supporting a wide range of forest ecosystem services (UNECE/FAO, 2018).

Employment and working conditions of the forest sector workforce have also undergone considerable change, reflecting a transformation in perception of occupational risks, health, safety but also wellbeing of forest workers over the last decades. Mechanization and digitalization have contributed to reduced accident rates, and increased productivity on sites where they could be deployed, while reducing the numbers of forest workers employed due to these new technologies.

Until recently, forest jobs mostly dealt with traditional silviculture and activities centred around timber harvest (classical forestry sector), which is still largely the public's perception of forest jobs. (UNECE/FAO, 2018). However, the nature of forest jobs is changing. UNECE/FAO (2018) identified seven areas where further development of jobs in the forest sector may occur, and listed examples of jobs in these areas – some better and some less well known (Figure 5.1).

What inferences about the outlook for the forest workforce can be drawn from the scenarios?

- Some of the options for adaptation to climate change involve silviculture which might be less suited to automation, especially thinning and harvesting (multi-species stands, single tree selection, or continuous cover).
- If there were a marked increase in forest area as modelled in the High Forest Area Scenario, a corresponding number of new jobs would have to be created, though the actual number would depend on the silvicultural choices made.
- Some of the disturbances linked to climate change would also have implications for working conditions. Fewer days with frozen soil complicate harvesting and could increase environmental damage through compaction. Salvage logging after insect outbreaks, storms or fires is hard and dangerous work and may well increase in frequency if the trend to more disturbance continues.

**FIGURE 5.1** SEVEN THEMATIC AREAS FOR FUTURE GREEN FOREST JOBS WITH CORRESPONDING EXAMPLES

| | |
|---|---|
| **Wood and Energy Production** | • Forest machine operator<br>• Log salvager<br>• Wood supply chain manager<br>• Local energy procurers<br>• Procurement forester<br>• Short rotation plantation manager |
| **Agroforestry and Mountain Forestry** | • Agro forester<br>• Project manager forests and natural hazards<br>• Project manager forest and protective structures<br>• Forest soil bioengineer<br>• Urban permaculturist<br>• Local natural hazard advisors |
| **Social and Urban Development** | • Forest historian<br>• Arboricultural officer<br>• Forest culture interpreter<br>• Funeral forest manager<br>• Urban forester<br>• Adventure park forester |
| **Forest Management, Inventory and Planning** | • Forest planner<br>• Forest inventory specialist<br>• Forest policy coordinator |
| **Biodiversity and Ecosystem Functioning** | • Forest wildlife manager<br>• Forest fire fighter<br>• Forest protection advocate and grassroots organizer |
| **Health and Recreation** | • Forest interpretive guide<br>• Forest ecotherapy guides |
| **Education and Research** | • Forest communicator<br>• Marketing and communication manager<br>• Forest pedagogue (teacher)<br>• Civil science facilitator |

**Source:** UNECE/FAO, 2018.

The forest workforce of tomorrow will rely on technology and organizational innovation, on establishment of rural and urban connections, on closer links with cross-cutting science such as natural resource management, landscape management and sustainable development as well as creating equal opportunities for women, young people and minority groups (UNECE/FAO, 2020a).

In the light of this increased scope of forest jobs, new skills will be required from forest workers. There has been concern about the challenge of attracting skilled, and particularly younger workers to jobs which are still often dangerous, physically hard, and with low social prestige. Further successful development of jobs will depend on the revision of existing curricula to address skill gaps and adapt to new career paths, and on lifelong learning opportunities for the forest sector workforce. In addition, continued work will be needed to raise awareness of existing and emerging job opportunities within the forest sector (UNECE/FAO, 2020b).

A study on trends in green jobs in the forest sector in the UNECE region (UNECE/FAO, 2020a) concluded, "green jobs have strong potential to contribute to rural development by retaining jobs in small- and medium-sized enterprises and offsetting job losses from mechanization, transitioning to a green economy. In addition, green jobs provide an opportunity to integrate young people and women into the forest sector workforce. [...] Continued work is needed to increase the awareness of existing and emerging green jobs within the forest sector and to ensure resilience and flexibility of the forest sector workforce. The economic, social and environmental benefits of forests in a green economy will heavily depend on society's ability to provide workers with the appropriate skills."

## 5.5 Women in the forest sector

Women are under-represented in the forest sector workforce. This is particularly the case for senior positions in private companies. However, there is a will to attract more women to forestry jobs and to achieve a better gender balance. Gender-relevant questions are addressed in international forest certification schemes. The Forest Stewardship Council (FSC) has requirements about maternity leave and reporting cases of gender-based discrimination and sexual harassment through a confidentiality mechanism. The Programme for the Endorsement of Forest Certification (PEFC) promotes gender equality and the role of women through a variety of requirements and processes. Forest managers must be committed to equal opportunities and non-discrimination, and gender equality promoted. Special consideration must be given to local people – women and men alike - for training and employment; wages, regardless of gender, must meet or exceed legal industry minimum standards.

Many women in forest companies are employed in administrative roles; studies point out that the pool of women qualified for leadership positions in the sector is still small (UNECE/FAO, 2020b). Recruiting younger employees and promoting them within organizations would address this issue. The numbers of women enrolled in forest faculties has been increasing since 2010 in many UNECE countries, a trend that is expected to continue. This may lead to more women being employed in the sector, especially in managerial positions, and in research.

## 5.6 Influence of pandemics on the forest sector outlook

By May 2021, the COVID-19 pandemic had infected over 160 million people worldwide and caused over three million deaths. In addition to the impacts on health, it has affected every part of society and the economy. Naturally, the forest sector has also felt its impacts. In the short term, there have been effects on supply and demand for products, trade patterns and supply chains, but it is not clear to what extent any of these are temporary or may persist as durable structural changes..

It has not been possible to incorporate the consequences of COVID-19 for the forest sector into the long-term scenarios. However, it is possible to speculate about possible long-term interactions of COVID-19 with the forest sector.

These are some of the questions which arise:

- Will the long-term growth rate of GDP – and thereby demand for forest products - resume its previous trend when this pandemic is under control?
- Will the relative competitiveness of different countries/ regions change? What effect might this have on trade flows, including for forest products?
- Will the recently-observed changes in consumer and producer behaviour, as a result of anti-COVID measures, such as the rise in e-commerce, working from home, reduced travel, increased video-conferencing, reduced tourism, and changing tourism patterns, persist in the longer term, and what might be the consequences for the forest sector?
- Will the drop in carbon emissions during this pandemic be maintained, changing both the climate change impacts on forests and the mitigation and adaptation challenges for the forest sector?
- Will the ongoing changes in the structure of supply chains, including for forest products, for reasons of resilience and security of supply, persist after this pandemic?
- Could forest management and the prevention of deforestation help in minimizing the risk of the transmission of diseases from animals to people at the wild/managed land interface?

# 6 Overview and food for further thought

## Background

- This chapter briefly summarizes the information on the background of the study and the reference scenario and then focuses on six priority questions which were identified through a transparent and participatory process.

I: How would different demand changes affect the UNECE forest products market?

II: How would different supply changes affect the UNECE region forest products markets?

III: How would significant trade restrictions affect the UNECE region forest product markets?

IV: How will UNECE forests be affected by climate change?

V: How could UNECE region forests and the forest sector contribute to climate change mitigation?

VI: How could UNECE forests adapt to climate change?

- Each of the six questions includes a short summary of the analysis of chapters 3 and 4.

- The final section briefly identifies, on the basis of the analysis in this study, some topics and questions which might be the subject of further thought and discussion, among those interested in the outlook for the forest sector in the UNECE region.

- It draws attention to a the following issues emerging from the analysis in the study, and asks questions which policy makers and stakeholders might consider.

  - Disturbances and the forest sink.
  - Demand for land for increased carbon sequestration by forests.
  - Putting substitution in a wider context.
  - Trade measures.
  - Need for a system-wide, holistic approach to strategies and policies.

## 6.1 Global trends and reference scenarios

In what type of world will the UNECE region forest sector develop to 2040? Of course, there is considerable uncertainty – exacerbated by the COVID-19 pandemic and its economic and social consequences – but some broad lines appear:

- Continuing economic growth, with a shift towards "emerging" markets and the east, driving demand for forest products.
- A potential slowdown in the growth of trade, possibly exacerbated by trade conflicts.
- Global population reaching 9.2 billion in 2040 according to UN projections, with strong growth in Africa, slower growth elsewhere, but a decline in Europe.
- An aging population in the UNECE region, with smaller households.
- Continuing urbanisation.
- Continuing decline in biodiversity, driven by changes in use of land and sea, overexploitation of natural resources, pollution and invasive species.
- New products and techniques, also for the forest sector.

The reference scenario assumes continuation of current market structures, and no shifts in policies, historical rates of technology change, and potential new products. It also assumes no change in climate conditions.[14] The broad features of the reference scenario are as follows:

- Rising per capita incomes are expected to lead to increasing total **forest area** through 2040 for Europe-EU, Europe-Other, the Russian Federation, and Eastern Europe, Caucasus and Central Asia (EECCA) and North America (the latter at a declining rate).
- Across all UNECE subregions, **forest growing stock** is projected to rise steadily from 2015 to 2040, continuing the patterns observed in the past. **Production capacity for industrial roundwood** also expands, having effects on production, consumption, trade, and prices of all forest products. However, outside the UNECE region, global growing stock continues its downward trend.
- Despite increasing forest growing stock, **primary and secondary product prices** are projected to increase in real terms. However, the price rises to 2040 are modest, remaining within the ranges of prices observed since 1990, indicating no substantial rise in wood scarcity.
- Production of **industrial roundwood** is projected to increase across all UNECE subregions and globally. Net exports also follow historical trends, with the EU projected to continue to remain a net importer and other UNECE subregions to remain net exporters of industrial roundwood.
- **Sawnwood** production is projected to rise most robustly in the EU, which is projected to be an increasingly important global source of sawnwood over the coming 20 years. North America, on the other hand, is projected to command a steadily smaller share of total UNECE and world output over time.
- Projections indicate rising total output of **wood-based panels** across all UNECE subregions, except North America, which is projected to have relatively stagnant total production.
- Projections for the **pulp and paper** sector show small to notable increases in wood pulp and paper production to 2040 in the UNECE region, as newsprint and printing and writing paper manufacturing continues its state of relative overall stagnation or decline in production and consumption, while other paper and paperboard continues to grow modestly, roughly in line with economic growth.
- Projected **consumption of forest products** generally follows trends in production despite increases in product prices.

## 6.2 Six key questions

### *I: How would different demand changes affect the UNECE forest products market?*

The forest sector, and many governments, are promoting increased use of wood, notably in construction, as a contribution to climate change mitigation and sustainable forest management, as well as for economic reasons. There are many opportunities for increased wood use in construction, notably through the substitution of new materials (CLT, LVL etc.) for non-wood materials. Will there be consequences for supply and demand for wood and perhaps even for sustainability of wood production? The scenarios explore and quantify these questions, first for an increase in demand outside the UNECE region, then for an increase in demand inside the UNECE region, then for a rise in demand from a new sector, wood-based textiles.

#### Increased wood-based construction in China

One of the megatrends described in chapter 2 shows a shift to the east – notably China – in economic growth. This scenario assumes that 10% of new housing units in China are of the same area and wood content found in the typical multifamily (apartment) dwelling in the US. If this occurs, the scenario projects (compared to the reference scenario):

- Increased harvests worldwide, but especially in China.

14 For full information on methods see chapter 3, and the methodology report available at https://unece.org/forests/forest-sector-outlook-study-fsos-2040.

- Marked increases in roundwood consumption and sawnwood production in China.
- More exports to China, from all parts of the UNECE region, of roundwood and sawnwood.
- Prices rise worldwide, especially for roundwood and sawnwood, and especially in China.
- More pressure on forest growing stock than in the reference scenario, but harvest still at sustainable levels (even in China).

### Increased wood-based construction in Europe and the Russian Federation

The shift to increasing consumption of sustainably produced forest products could come about through any of a combination of avenues, including changes in international building standards to allow for larger and taller wood-frame structures, increased acceptance by the architectural design community, builders, and property owners of mass timber products, including cross-laminated timber (CLT), glulam beams, etc. and policies and programs designed to favour wood over non-wood construction inputs as a way of mitigating climate change. This scenario therefore assumes that wood (sawnwood and panels) consumption in Europe and the Russian Federation increases to the same (high) levels as in North America at present. If this occurs, the scenario projects (relative to the reference scenario):

- Higher harvests worldwide, not only in Europe/Russia, although increases would be considerably less than in the first scenario.
- Higher production and consumption of roundwood, sawnwood and panels in Europe, and decreased net exports to satisfy higher European demand.
- In Russia, however, roundwood production is slightly higher than in the reference scenario, but sawnwood production lower, as the Russian Federation exports its roundwood to other regions and imports more sawnwood.
- North American consumption is slightly lower than in the reference scenario, but its production and exports increase strongly, as it responds to the demand in Europe and Russia
- Prices rise marginally, worldwide, for roundwood and derived wood products.
- Forest growing stock does not drop in absolute terms but is slightly lower than in the reference scenario.

### Increased production of wood-based textiles

Considerable interest has been expressed in new outlets for wood, for commercial reasons, and to replace more carbon intensive products, such as oil-based textiles. There has been considerable research and development, as well as investment, sometimes supported by governments. This what-if scenario explores the consequences if the textile sector, by 2040, replaced 30% of its fibre intake with wood-based fibres. If this occurs, the scenario projects:

- Roundwood production worldwide would be slightly higher than in the reference scenario, and forest growing stock marginally lower – but still higher than in the base year.
- Sawnwood production in the UNECE region would be notably lower as a reaction to higher wood prices and other structural shifts. Lower UNECE production would be partially compensated by higher production elsewhere notably in China.
- Panel production in the UNECE region would be slightly lower than in the reference scenario, with reduced net export.
- UNECE region net exports of sawnwood and panels would be lower than in the reference scenario, while China's net exports of sawnwood would be higher/net imports would be lower.
- The Russian Federation would significantly increase its net exports of industrial roundwood.

It should be noted that these projections are subject to caution as the GFPM is not designed to follow the interactions between supply and demand of residues and recycled wood.

## *II: How would different supply changes affect the UNECE region forest products markets?*

Changes in the supply of roundwood would affect world markets. Such changes might occur through government action, or demand pressure, for instance rising population or economic growth. In particular, many governments have put in place measures to increase forest area, notably to respond to Target 1.1 of the United Nations Strategic Plan for Forests (UNSPF), ("Forest area is increased by 3 per cent worldwide" by 2030). Also, there is rising concern about the consequences of forest disturbances, including fire, insects, storms etc. on forest ecosystems and their capacity to produce wood on a sustainable basis. Many governments and stakeholders are also committed under the Bonn Challenge to restore degraded forests. The scenarios explore and quantify these questions, first for a significant expansion of global forest area then for an increase in planted forest area outside the UNECE region, and finally in a context of changing disturbance regimes.

### Increased global forest area

There is widespread interest in expanding forest area, to satisfy demand for wood, notably in areas of fast economic growth and growing population, to reverse deforestation and to mitigate climate change. This scenario explores what might happen if forest area worldwide expanded by 10% by 2040. If this occurs, the scenario projects:

- Harvest of industrial roundwood world-wide would be higher than in the reference scenario, while growing stock would be even higher, over 10% more than in the reference scenario.
- Increased of forest growing stocks lowers prices for both roundwood and forest products, and thereby causes production and consumption of roundwood and products to increase, in all regions.
- Roundwood prices are lower than those in the reference scenario by about 3% and prices of products lower by 0.5-1.7%.

### Increased planted forest area outside the UNECE region

Planted forests are driven by different factors than natural forests: in recent years, an increasing share of wood production has come from planted forests. All scenarios in this study projected both natural forest and planted forest area. A recent paper (Nepal *et al.*, 2019b), also based on the GFPM, and summarised in Chapter 3, compared a scenario without the natural/planted distinction with another where more than 77% of the projected global expansion in planted area by 2040 occurred outside the UNECE region. If this occurs, the scenario projects:

- Forest growing stock worldwide would be 2% higher than in the reference scenario.
- Prices would decrease for industrial roundwood and wood products.
- Global production and consumption for all products would increase.
- Industrial roundwood production would increase, in particular in Africa and Asia.

### Increased rate of natural disturbances

The effects of natural disturbances on markets are often random, local and short term in nature, and thereby difficult to model over long time periods. However, some conclusions are possible about the forest product market effects of disturbances over the coming 25 years in the UNECE region:

- A part of the roundwood entering the market will emanate from salvage activities; this part will vary over time;
- If the share of this salvage volume increases, it would tend to dampen roundwood prices, locally and possibly nationally; if it falls, prices would strengthen;
- If mortality increases because of disturbances, constraining wood supply, this would lead to longer-run price enhancements when the disturbance is large relative to total growing stock;
- Although the effects of such disturbances on forest resources might be profound at national and subnational scales, global forest products markets would tend to register only dampened effects of those disturbances, as trade adjusts supply at a global level – at least within the range of disturbance which has been the subject of quantified analysis.

### *III: How would significant trade restrictions affect the UNECE region forest product markets?*

Over past decades, tariff and non-tariff barriers to trade in forest products, like all goods, have been steadily reduced, as markets and supply chains became global. However, in recent years, a number of trade disputes have arisen, inside and outside the UNECE region, for forest products as for other products. There have been increased restrictions on some trade flows, for instance on sawnwood, industrial wood (export bans), recovered paper, and other products. These have raised questions about the long-term consequences of such restrictions, on countries and products directly affected and on global markets, over a longer period. Also, the consequences are very different for producers, and consumers, who often have opposing interests.

Buongiorno and Johnston (2018) analysed the consequences of tariffs imposed by the US, and of retaliation by other countries to these tariffs based on an analysis with the GFPM. Their conclusions should be broadly valid in other trade situations. The authors found that:

- With the United States import restrictions and no retaliation by trading partners, the welfare of the United States producers would rise but by less than the losses experienced by the United States consumers, due to higher domestic (US) prices and lower the United States consumption. Outside the United States, producers would lose more than consumers gain.
- With retaliatory measures imposed by trading partners against products from the United States, the results were different. Within the United States, welfare of the United States consumers rose due to lower prices and higher consumption, but their gains were outweighed by the United States producer losses. In the rest of the world under that second simulation (i.e. restrictions plus retaliation), consumer welfare decreased more than producer welfare increased, also a net loss.

In short, this analysis confirms that trade disputes that involve duelling measures and countermeasures would cause decreased overall welfare (producer and consumer surplus) in the forest sector.

### *IV: How will UNECE forests be affected by climate change?*

Climate change and forest ecosystems are both extremely complex. Nevertheless, on the basis of a review of the literature, it is possible to say:

- In several parts of the UNECE region – but by no means everywhere - climate change appears to have increased the **productivity** of forests. However, it is highly uncertain how long these positive effects on productivity will continue in the future until they are limited by physiological constraints, or availability of phosphorus, nitrogen or water. Mediterranean forests are already at risk of climate induced productivity losses and similar questions are arising in other regions. In general, there may be more variability of productivity over time due to direct or lagged effects of extreme events. Furthermore, changes in forest productivity do not necessarily translate into availability of high-quality timber.
- As climate changes, **species distribution ranges** and the associated forest types are moving towards the poles and higher elevations. There is concern that the migration speed of many tree species may not be able to keep up with the changing climatic conditions and that the receding edges of species distribution ranges are often characterised by strong susceptibility to disturbances like drought, pathogens and insects.
- In forest ecosystems, **disturbances** such as wind, drought, fire, and insect outbreaks generate a heterogeneous landscape and promote forest rejuvenation. Since the early 1970s, forest disturbances have increased in number and severity and are expected to continue to do so in the future. Disturbance agents also rarely occur alone but often act in combination with each other. The main disturbances and the outlook for them are briefly described below:
    - Susceptibility of forest stands to **wind** damage is strongly linked to wind properties, stand characteristics, forest management and site conditions. Thinning can increase stand resistance to wind damage, although there is a short-lived interval of increased vulnerability after the thinning operation. Enhanced forest productivity, increased winter precipitation and the lack of soil frost, all associated with climate change, may increase the impact of storms, which cause significant and long-lasting economic damage in the region affected, even if the market effects are absorbed at the global level quite rapidly.
    - **Droughts** have increased in number, severity and duration since the beginning of the twentieth century, with substantial impacts on forests. Moreover, climate models project that this trend will continue. In addition, consecutive drought events progressively reduce tree health and increase susceptibility to other disturbance agents.
    - **Fire**[15] is recognised as the primary driver of forest dynamics in boreal and Mediterranean forests, although it has been marginalised in temperate forests in Europe. As a result of rising temperatures and shifts in precipitation, drier weather conditions have been occurring more often, which, combined with increasing amounts of fuel wood and a higher lightning activity, are expected to increase the number, size and intensity of fires. Significant damage from fire – loss of human life, reduced value of growing stock, economic disruption, reduction of other forest benefits - is reported all over the UNECE region.
    - Climate change directly influences the survival and metabolic rate of **insects and pathogens**. Warmer and wetter climate conditions are expected to facilitate activity and abundance of pathogens. Warmer and drier climate conditions are lessening the natural defences of trees to thwart attacks, significantly increasing the spatial extent and duration of outbreaks of insects. The dry European summer of 2018 enabled bark beetles to complete a third reproduction cycle, causing an unprecedented outbreak in Central Europe. The mountain pine beetle outbreak in British Columbia and Alberta spread over 18 million hectares and destroyed a merchantable timber volume of 752 million $m^3$.
    - Accumulating **snow and ice** on tree crowns can lead to breakage, and subsequently influence forest functioning. In combination with a lack of frozen soil and wind storms, heavy ice and snow loads can also cause uprooting of trees. Ice storms occur at low frequencies but have a strong impact on forests when they occur. Disturbances from snow and ice are difficult to project and may regionally either increase or decrease under climate change.
- **Harvesting operations** in boreal and many temperate forests are historically carried out during winter, as the increased bearing capacity of frozen soils results in higher efficiency of forest machines, reduced soil damage and lower risks for forest workers. The changes in winter conditions as a result of climate change (reduction of number of days with frozen soils) might lead to a cascading set of problems for commercial and precommercial logging, for mobilizing timber all year round and for maintaining a steady demand for labour.

A scenario explored the consequences for global wood markets of increased net primary productivity of forests due to climate change (without taking account of the possible restrictions

15 This does not include prescribed burning, considered a part of forest management. Fires may be caused by humans (accidental or intentional) or be natural, notably because of lightning. The share of different causes varies widely between parts of the UNECE region.

on increased productivity mentioned above). Increased net primary productivity resulted in higher forest stocks, and thereby reduced prices for roundwood and products in all countries, and higher production and consumption. These developments significantly altered the comparative advantage of producing and consuming countries, causing diverging trends in different countries and regions.

### *V: How could UNECE region forests and the forest sector contribute to climate change mitigation?*

The forest sector can contribute to climate change mitigation in three ways: carbon sequestration in forests, carbon storage in harvested wood products, and avoidance of emissions from fossil based or energy intensive materials and fuels (substitution). The study attempts to explore and quantify the importance of these different pathways. The reference scenario under the GFPM assumes no new policy or technical measures to increase mitigation but nevertheless projects significant contributions of forests to climate change mitigation: an increase in carbon stocks, in forests, and in products. All UNECE subregions represent a net carbon sink during the projection period, for a total of around 1.5 billion $tCO_2e$ per year in the reference scenarios, although at the global level, the net sink was lower - about 1.2 billion $tCO_2e$ per year - as forests in Africa, South America and Oceania represent a net source. For harvested wood products, the annual sink over the projection period in the reference scenario was about 0.5 billion $tCO_2e$.

The study explores the options for increasing the contribution UNECE region forests could make to mitigating climate change. This is summarised below.

**Changes in forest management** include changes in species (faster growing species) and silvicultural regimes (longer rotations, different thinning regimes), and above all, reductions in the level of harvest. These changes would all increase the forest sink in the UNECE region, although the quantitative estimates vary widely. Likewise, if harvests were to increase, the carbon stock in forest biomass would be lower than it would otherwise have been. It should also be pointed out that an increased level of disturbance could counteract these measures to increase carbon sequestration through forest management.

**Afforestation and reforestation**, in particular combined with long term carbon storage,[16] is assessed by the IPCC, as a prerequisite for achieving the objectives of the Paris Agreement. In 2019, the IPCC special report on climate change and land considered that expanding global forest area by 1 billion ha would be an economically effective way of advancing towards the target of limiting climate change to 1.5°C above preindustrial levels by 2100. The major challenges to achieving this are finding sufficient appropriate land, and financial resources as well as creating the necessary policy and governance framework for such a major change in land use: a 25% increase in forest area. The High Forest Area scenario, prepared using the GFPM for this study, assumed a less ambitious increase, of 10% in global forest area by 2040, which translates into a sixfold increase in carbon sequestration by forests. This extra sequestration would make a significant contribution to mitigation (compensating nearly 4% of emissions) but would require 180-320 million ha of plantations, and a reversal of recent trends in forest area.

Mitigation strategies focussing on increased use of wood products rely on a combination of an **increased carbon pool in harvested wood products (HWP) and avoidance of emissions** from materials which are fossil-based (e.g. plastic and polyester) or energy-intensive (e.g., concrete, steel, glass). However, while progress has been made on determining the size and changes in the HWP carbon pool, as reported above, determination of the magnitudes of substitution effects remains still a challenging research undertaking. Chapter 4 examined the carbon-related aspects of the two scenarios in chapter 3 based on assumption of higher wood consumption. Both showed that more carbon was sequestered in HWP than in the reference scenario and that more GHG emissions by fossil fuels and energy intensive materials were avoided than in the reference scenario. However, to achieve these results, it was necessary to increase harvests of industrial wood, and thus bring the forest biomass carbon stock below what it would otherwise have been. The two effects roughly counterbalance each other at the global level through 2040, although there are some significant geographical shifts in emissions and carbon flows.

Another substitution strategy is to increase the use of wood to make **textiles** to replace fossil-based and energy intensive textile feedstocks. The increased use of wood fibres for textiles avoided global emissions of 77 million $tCO_2e$ per year and sequestered an extra 5.4 million $tCO_2e$ per year in HWP. However, carbon sequestration in forests was lower than in the reference scenario, and non-wood alternatives outside textiles also increased, so that this scenario is only nearly carbon neutral at the global level.

**Wood energy** accounts for more than half of renewable energy produced in the UNECE region. The sustainability and overall benefits of biomass energy are the subject of intense policy debate, which cannot be summarised here. The uncertainties and interactions are complex, but a few main insights have been identified:

- Use of forest bioenergy reduces fossil fuel use and long-term carbon emission impacts, provided forest area and forest biomass stock do not decrease.
- Increasing demand for wood for energy provides economic incentives (higher timber prices) for investments in forestry,

16 Either in forest biomass or other forms of storage, including carbon capture after burning.

potentially leading to increased forest area and higher forest productivity.

- Although bioenergy from wood contributes to increased emissions in the short-term, the long-term cumulative biogenic $CO_2$ emissions are reduced by substituting forest bioenergy for fossil fuels – although this substitution effect will diminish as renewable energies account for a larger part of energy supply.

Demand for energy wood is driven to a significant extent by policy: the EU has ambitious targets to increase the share of renewable energy, including from wood. EFSOS II in 2010 concluded that it was possible to provide the very large supplementary volumes of wood for energy called for by EU policy makers, but only if energy efficiency was improved and all biomass sources were mobilised, but that there would be significant trade-offs, notably as regards land-use and biodiversity.

### *VI: How could UNECE forests adapt to climate change?*

Adapting forests to climate change involves adjusting forest ecosystem management in order to reduce negative impacts and to use the opportunities which arise. Adaptation can happen through natural processes, such as genetic selection, or through management by humans. Adaptive forest management uses ecological understanding regarding future climate change impacts to create a resilient forest, one that is able to cope with a range of future conditions while still providing the main services requested by society. Given the uncertainty about future climate and about forest ecosystems' reaction to the changed circumstances, the effectiveness of management choices must be monitored and strategies adapted if necessary.

The measures to be taken vary widely according to the circumstances of each forest stand, its site characteristics, possible future climate and management objectives. Managers may take a reactive or a proactive approach and may act on different timescales and geographic range (stand, landscape, national policy/governance). General recommendations for proactive adaptation aim to reduce risks as far as possible and spread the remaining risks among stand members. More efforts are needed to prevent or mitigate future disturbance impacts and to be better prepared to manage unavoidable risks.

At the stand level, there are many possible opportunities, including:

- at the regeneration stage, changing species composition and structure, preferring natural or enriched natural regeneration;
- modifying thinning regimes to improve resilience
- converting the forest type, although this may be a very long process
- post-disturbance salvage logging, sanitary fellings and plantings to guide future stand development.

Beyond the stand level, it may be desirable to adapt policy and governance, for instance by adapting the decision-making processes to the changing circumstances, possibly by allowing decision making at a more local level, putting in place long term arrangements between forest owners and processing industries.

Hence, effective adaptation requires a set of policies and measures that can deal with the immediate response actions as well as the long term proactive/preparatory actions. Specific instruments could address the suitability of reproductive materials in a changing climate, and the difficulty of relying on natural forest restoration processes after disturbance. This requires a wide set of measures and policies which take into account the needs of other concerned sectors, such as biodiversity, energy, tourism, rural development or mitigation of climate change.

Furthermore, adaptation of forest management to climate change is often part of wider national strategies of adaptation to climate change, in accordance with the provisions of the UN Framework Convention for Climate Change. The national strategies can play an important role, not only in coordinating forest related measures with other measures, but also in channelling resources and political will towards forest management actions.

## 6.3 Food for further thought

This study has shown that the forest sector is facing new conditions, notably of climate, new challenges and new expectations from society and outlined possible consequences of certain policy choices and external events, as a support for evidence-based policy making. It does not claim to forecast the future, or to recommend any policy or management choices. However, some of the analysis has thrown a light on possible future developments and choices which might be of interest to policy makers. This final section briefly identifies, on the basis of the analysis in this study, some topics and questions which might be the subject of further thought and discussion, among those interested in the outlook for the forest sector in the UNECE region. It draws attention to a few issues emerging from the analysis in the study, and asks questions which policy makers and stakeholders might consider.

### *6.3.1 Disturbances and the forest sink*

#### *Outlook*

The UNECE region forests are a carbon sink – and will continue to be one in all scenarios, whatever the projected harvest level, forest area etc. However there have been major disturbances in recent years, notably insect outbreaks in Central Europe (bark beetles), British Columbia and Oregon (mountain pine beetle) as well as fires in western north America, the southern and eastern Mediterranean and Siberia. These disturbances release the carbon sequestered by the forest, back to the atmosphere, and are difficult to foresee, prevent or control. The amount of carbon emitted during these disturbances is roughly comparable to the forest sink (see Table 4.7). Disturbances, especially storms, fires and insect infestations, are expected to become more frequent and serious as the climate changes. The scenarios for the forest sink presented in the outlook cannot take increased disturbances into account, as it was not possible to project stochastic events like natural disturbances with the analytical tools available.[17] There is therefore a risk that the mitigation effect of the forest sink could be counteracted, in whole or in part, by the emissions caused by disturbances.

#### Food for thought

The study shows that, for the forest sector, mitigation of and adaptation to climate change are intimately linked, although they are often analysed using different tools and by different specialisations,[18] linked by the carbon balance. Furthermore, the time horizons for the different events and strategies vary widely, from the very short term, like some disturbances, to the very long term, notably silvicultural rotations and ecological adaptation. The challenge facing the sector as a whole is to combine strategies to increase the forest sink with strategies to reduce the risk of natural disturbances, taking account of the risk inherent in both adaptation and mitigation. There might also be trade-offs between creating the maximum carbon sink (e.g. by using fast growing species and intensive silviculture) and improving resilience (e.g. by establishing mixed species, mixed-age stands, with a more extensive silvicultural approach).

#### Questions

*How to combine mitigation and adaptation strategies, addressing the short, medium and long term?*

*What silvicultural solutions minimise risk while optimising both mitigation and resilience, over the whole cycle?*

*How to measure and monitor disturbance and resilience in the forest sector?*

### 6.3.2 Demand for land for increased carbon sequestration by forests

#### Outlook

Increased carbon sequestration, including by forests, plays a major role in all strategies for climate change mitigation. For instance, the IPCC special report on climate change and land considered that expanding global forest area by 1 billion ha could advance towards the target of limiting climate change to 1.5°C above preindustrial levels by 2100. The consequences for the global forest sector of increased forest area were explored in two scenarios of this study (see sections 3.5.1 and 3.5.2 and 4.3.2). However, the increase in area modelled in these scenarios, 397-493 million ha, was less than half what was proposed by the IPCC. The scenarios projected increased harvests and consumption of wood, and lower prices, as well as a significant increase in carbon sequestration, but did not take increased natural disturbances into account.

#### Food for thought

If it were decided to expand forest area globally by a billion hectares, or even 400 million ha (25% and 10% respectively of global forest area in 2020), there would be many challenges, of land availability, of silviculture, of social adaptation and land tenure, of financial resources and of forest management objectives. Much land is not available for large scale afforestation, as it is infertile (mountains, deserts etc.), urbanised, strictly protected for biodiversity conservation or already with forest cover. Most available land would be marginal land (with its own values for extensive agriculture, landscape, recreation etc.) and agricultural land.

#### Questions

*Is it possible to increase forest area by the amounts called for in the climate strategies? And, if so, what are the main challenges and how might they be overcome?*

*How much land is realistically available in the UNECE region for mitigation of climate change, taking account of the constraints and trade-offs described above?*

*How to decide whether carbon sequestration is the most appropriate use of a particular area, compared to, say, agriculture? How to resolve the inevitable conflicts and trade-offs which would accompany such a significant change in land use?*

*How can forest managers find the optimum balance between carbon accumulation and wood production, as well as avoiding emissions during and after the rotation?*

### 6.3.3 Putting substitution in a wider context

#### Outlook

Using sustainably produced forest products instead of carbon-intensive materials such as cement or plastics may avoid significant emissions. The scenarios in this study show that increased consumption of forest products, including for substitution, avoids emissions from carbon intensive materials. However, this pathway also reduces the global forest biomass carbon stock (compared to what it would have been without substitution), by roughly equivalent amounts (section 4.5).

---

17 See discussion in section 3.5.3.

18 For instance, in this study, by modelling and projection for the forest sink, and by analysis of stand behaviour for the adaptation of forests to climate change.

There is also significant leakage of emissions between regions: the avoided emissions tend to be in the region where substitution takes place while the lower-than-expected growing stock tends to be elsewhere. Thus, the mitigation effect of substitution, at the global level, is lower if resulting changes in the forest growing stock are taken into account. In one scenario, increased substitution led to no significant change in the sink at the level of the global carbon balance (see section 4.3.2).

### Food for thought

The avoided emissions (substitution factors) depend crucially on the detail of the substitution: what is substituted, by what? All elements of this equation matter. In particular, using sustainable wood to substitute for very carbon intensive materials and uses will avoid more emissions than using the same wood to substitute for less carbon intensive materials and uses. On the other side of the equation, if the wood-based pathway has the minimum possible carbon emissions, the avoided emissions will also be higher than if there are significant carbon emissions over the life cycle. This implies that the wood-based pathways should not only be based on sustainably produced wood, but also have minimum waste at all stages, and the most carbon-efficient production processes, logistical solutions and construction techniques possible. Thus, substitution is not a simple question of using wood rather than another material, but of using highly carbon efficient wood-based pathways to substitute for the most carbon intensive pathways. This aspect should also be taken into consideration when designing strategies - although it may be difficult to incorporate such detailed and site-specific considerations into broader policy documents.

As a first step, when drawing up strategies, policy makers may wish to consider, as this study has done, the consequences of their choices for the global carbon balance, not just for avoiding emissions. Some measures can improve the net balance of substitution: producing, manufacturing and using forest products in the most carbon-efficient way possible will increase the substitution effect, as will substituting the most carbon rich materials and uses. More precise "targeting" of substitution could thus improve the overall mitigation effect.

### Questions

*How to develop strategies which both encourage substitution for carbon-rich materials and minimise reduction to the forest growing stock?*

*Which carbon intensive products and pathways might be substituted by wood-based products and pathways to get the most avoided emissions?*

*How to minimise carbon emissions in the value chain of the wood products which substitute for carbon intensive materials?*

*How to encourage the circular use of wood and forest products, including repurposing, re-use and recycling? What are the best strategies and how should progress be monitored?*

## 6.3.4 Trade measures

### Outlook

Trade in roundwood and forest products has been rising, like all trade, over recent decades and is projected to continue to increase. In the UNECE region, for trade in forest products, a few tariffs are in place, along with a number of non-tariff measures, including phytosanitary regulations, but also measures to prevent imports of illegally or unsustainably produced forest products. Examples of the latter are the EU Timber Regulation and the United States Lacey Act. Under discussion in a number of forums, notably the EU, are measures to limit imports of products linked with deforestation (not only forest products) or where originating countries are considered to have infringed international conventions, on environment and social governance, for instance violating International Labour Organization (ILO) Codes of Practice or international human rights instruments. These "environmental social and governance" (ESG) measures could well also affect trade in wood and forest products. Emission linked measures are also under discussion, notably the EU proposal for a carbon border adjustment mechanism.[19] One FSOS scenario (see section 3.6) demonstrated that overall welfare (as defined in traditional economic terms) is reduced by restrictions on trade (only tariffs in this scenario), although any trade measure creates both winners and losers. However, the proposed, non-tariff measures, if implemented as proposed, would create a new framework for international trade, imposing new procedures (not yet accounted for in the existing WTO framework for world trade) and changing – positively or negatively - the competitivity and market access of all those trading in wood and forest products. The implications of these proposed, but not yet widely applied, measures were not analysed in FSOS.

### Food for thought

The global trading system for forest products may be about to experience fundamental change with the arrival of a new "layer" of ESG-focused trade measures of the type outlined above, which have not, so far, been considered in global outlook studies. This raises a number of fundamental questions, about avoiding protectionism, using trade measures to achieve non-trade (ESG) objectives, and the possible resulting changes in the competitive positions of trading countries.

19 At present, forest products are not included in this measure, which focuses on a few carbon intensive materials and energies (iron and steel, cement, fertiliser, aluminium and electricity generation). However, given the carbon emissions linked to deforestation, forest products might be included at a later stage.

### Questions

*How to use the developing trading system to promote sustainable forest management worldwide, and the achievement of the Sustainable Development Goals?*

*How to ensure that the non-tariff measures, including existing measures to promote SFM as well as phytosanitary measures and the new generation of "ESG" measures, are not merely protectionist in effect, excluding certain countries or products from certain markets?*

*What would be the long-term consequences of these changes to the rules of the international trading system for the forest sector of the UNECE region?*

*What would be the consequences for the forest sector if these types of measures were only adapted in certain regions (e.g. the UNECE region) and not worldwide?*

## 6.3.5 Need for a system-wide, holistic approach to strategies and policies

### Outlook

This study has shown that there are consequences of structural changes, climate change and the resulting policy choices in other regions and other parts of the sector, and even to global carbon balances. Examples of these global interactions are the effect of substitution on the net carbon balance, and the effects on trade and production worldwide of increased consumption of forest products in one part of the world. In fact, the global forest sector itself is only a subsystem of even larger systems, notably the planet's climate, and this must be borne in mind too, although analysis has its limits.

### Food for thought

Given the importance of international trade and globalisation, not to mention the global interactions of the carbon cycle, analysis based on a less than complete vision of the forest sector worldwide may be considered potentially misleading, if it fails to take a holistic approach. There is a need to consider all aspects together (from forest to recycling and final disposal of products, from plantation to regeneration, over the whole world), because of the leakages and consequences in other regions demonstrated by the modelling. In general, a system approach is needed to properly understand the outlook

In the past the common unit was m$^3$ of wood (question posed: will there be "enough wood"?), now tons of carbon (tons of $CO_2$ equivalent) must be added (question posed: "what is the effect of policy choices on the overall carbon balance?") if the full picture is to become apparent

Nevertheless, global models, which must simplify reality, have their drawbacks, and many aspects are difficult to analyse in a global system perspective. The challenge is to continue to find and use the linkages between the global system perspective and the very local perspective which is essential to understanding forest ecosystems.

Furthermore, forest policy and decision making are made at the stand or national level, and there are few mechanisms of consultation and co-decision whereby the insights from a system-wide analysis can be implemented at the local or national level.

### Questions

*How to develop analytical tools which reconcile the complexities of a system approach with the local realities of forest management and national or subnational policy formulation?*

*How to help national and subnational policy makers take into account the system approach?*

# References

All references can be found online at:

https://unece.org/forestry-timber/documents/2022/04/informal-documents/references-fsos-2020-2040

SCAN ME

# Annexes

# ANNEX 1: COUNTRIES IN THE UNECE REGION AND ITS SUBREGIONS

**Eastern Europe, Caucasus and Central Asia**

Armenia
Azerbaijan
Belarus
Georgia
Kazakhstan
Kyrgyzstan
Republic of Moldova
Russian Federation
Tajikistan
Turkmenistan
Ukraine
Uzbekistan

**North America**

Canada
United States of America

**European Union**

Austria
Belgium
Bulgaria
Croatia
Cyprus
Czech Republic
Denmark
Estonia
Finland
France
Germany
Greece
Hungary
Ireland
Italy
Latvia
Lithuania
Luxembourg
Malta
Netherlands
Poland
Portugal
Romania
Slovakia
Slovenia
Spain
Sweden

**Europe other countries**

Albania
Andorra
Bosnia and Herzegovina
Iceland
Israel
Liechtenstein
Monaco
Montenegro
North Macedonia
Norway
San Marino
Serbia
Switzerland
Turkey
United Kingdom of Great Britain and Northern Ireland

# ANNEX 2: LIST OF AUTHORS AND CONTRIBUTORS

## AUTHORS

| Given name | Family name | Chapter(s) | Affiliation | Email address |
|---|---|---|---|---|
| Galina | Churkina | 4 | Potsdam Institute for Climate Impact Research | Galina.Churkina@pik-potsdam.de |
| Mariana | Hassegawa | 4 | European Forest Institute | mariana.hassegawa@efi.int |
| Tristan | Herrmann | 2 | Hohenheim University | tristan.herrmann@uni-hohenheim.de |
| Louis | König | 4 | Wageningen University | louis.konig@wur.nl |
| Prakash | Nepal | 3, 4 | USDA Forest Service | prakash.nepal@usda.gov |
| Jeffrey | Prestemon | 3, 4 | USDA Forest Service | Jeffrey.Prestemon@usda.gov |
| Christopher | Prins | 1, 2, 4, 5, 6 | Independen Consultant | kit.prins@gmail.com |
| Christopher P.O. | Reyer | 4 | Potsdam Institute for Climate Impact Research | reyer@pik-potsdam.de |
| Mart-Jan | Schelhaas | 4 | Wageningen University | martjan.schelhaas@wur.nl |
| Pieter Johannes | Verkerk | 4 | European Forest Institute | hans.verkerk@efi.int |

## CONTRIBUTORS

| Given name | Family name | Affiliation |
|---|---|---|
| Elias | Hurmekoski | University of Helsinki |
| Ragnar | Jonsson | Swedish University of Agricultural Sciences |
| John | Kim | USDA Forest Service |
| Marcus | Lindner | European Forest Institute |
| Gert-Jan | Nabuurs | Wageningen University |

## ANNEX 3: SOME FACTS ABOUT THE EUROPEAN FORESTRY COMMISSION

The European Forestry Commission (EFC), which was created in 1947, is one of six regional forestry commissions established by FAO to provide a policy and technical forum for countries to discuss and address forest issues on a regional basis.

The purpose of the EFC is to advise on the formulation of forest policies and to review and coordinate their implementation at the regional level; exchange information; advise on suitable practices and actions to address technical and economic problems (generally through special subsidiary bodies); and make appropriate recommendations in relation to the foregoing. The EFC meets every two years and its official languages are English, French and Spanish.

The EFC has a number of associated subsidiary bodies, including the Working Party on the Management of Mountain Watersheds; the UNECE/FAO Working Party on Forest Statistics, Economics and Management; and seven UNECE/FAO Teams of Specialists. The Committee on Mediterranean Forestry Issues (Silva Mediterranea) informs the EFC.

FAO encourages the wide participation of government officials from forestry and other sectors as well as representatives of international, regional and subregional organizations that deal with forest-related issues in the region, including non-governmental organizations and the private sector. Accordingly, the EFC is open to all members and associate members whose territories are situated wholly or in part in the European Region or who are responsible for the international relations of any non-self-governing territory in that region. Membership comprises such eligible member nations as have notified the Director-General of their desire to be considered as members.

The EFC is one of the technical commissions serving the FAO Regional Office for Europe and Central Asia (REU), and the EFC Secretary is based in Geneva. EFC work is regulated by its Rules of Procedures, which were adopted by the FAO Conference in 1961 and amended at the Eighteenth Session of the EFC in 1977.

## ANNEX 4: SOME FACTS ABOUT THE COMMITTEE ON FORESTS AND THE FOREST INDUSTRY

The UNECE Committee on Forests and the Forest Industry (COFFI) is a principal subsidiary body of the UNECE based in Geneva. It constitutes a forum for cooperation and consultation between member countries on forestry, the forest industry and forest product matters. All countries of Europe and the EECCA, as well as the United States, Canada and Israel, are members of the UNECE and participate in its work.

The UNECE Committee on Forests and the Forest Industry shall, within the context of sustainable development, provide member countries with the information and services needed for policymaking and decision-making with regard to their forest and forest industry sectors, including the trade and use of forest products and, where appropriate, it will formulate recommendations addressed to member governments and interested organizations. To this end, it shall:

1. with the active participation of member countries, undertake short-, medium- and long-term analyses of developments in, and having an impact on, the sector, including those developments offering possibilities for facilitating international trade and for enhancing the protection of the environment;
2. lin support of these analyses, collect, store and disseminate statistics relating to the sector, and carry out activities to improve their quality and comparability;
3. provide a framework for cooperation, for example by organizing seminars, workshops and ad hoc meetings and setting up time-limited ad hoc groups, for the exchange of economic, environmental and technical information between governments and other institutions of member countries required for the development and implementation of policies leading to the sustainable development of the sector and the protection of the environment in their respective countries;
4. carry out tasks identified by the UNECE or the Committee on Forests and the Forest Industry as being of priority, including the facilitation of subregional cooperation and activities in support of the economies in transition of central and eastern Europe and of the countries of the region that are developing from an economic perspective; and
5. keep under review its structure and priorities and cooperate with other international and intergovernmental organizations active in the sector, particularly FAO and its European Forestry Commission and the International Labour Organization, in order to ensure complementarity and avoid duplication, thereby optimizing the use of resources.

***More information about the work of the EFC and COFFI may be obtained by contacting:***

UNECE/FAO Forestry and Timber Section
Forests, Land and Housing Division
United Nations Economic Commission for Europe/
Food and Agriculture Organization of the United Nations
Palais des Nations
CH-1211 Geneva 10, Switzerland

**info.ECE-FAOforests@un.org**

**www.unece.org/forests**

# ANNEX 5: UNECE/FAO PUBLICATIONS

**Geneva Timber and Forest Study Papers**

| | |
|---|---|
| Forest Products Annual Market Review 2019-2020 | ECE/TIM/SP/50 |
| Forests in a Circular Economy | ECE/TIM/SP/49 |
| Forest Products Annual Market Review 2018-2019 | ECE/TIM/SP/48 |
| State of Forests of the Caucasus and Central Asia | ECE/TIM/SP/47 |
| Forest Products Annual Market Review 2017-2018 | ECE/TIM/SP/46 |
| Forests and Water | ECE/TIM/SP/44 |
| Forest Ownership in the ECE Region | ECE/TIM/SP/43 |
| Wood Energy in the ECE Region | ECE/TIM/SP/42 |
| Forest Products Annual Market Review 2016-2017 | ECE/TIM/SP/41 |
| Forest Products Annual Market Review 2015-2016 | ECE/TIM/SP/40 |
| Forest Products Annual Market Review 2014-2015 | ECE/TIM/SP/39 |
| Promoting sustainable building materials and the implications on the use of wood in buildings | ECE/TIM/SP/38 |
| Forests in the ECE Region: Trends and Challenges in Achieving the Global Objectives on Forests | ECE/TIM/SP/37 |
| Forest Products Annual Market Review 2013-2014 | ECE/TIM/SP/36 |
| Rovaniemi Action Plan for the Forest Sector in a Green Economy | ECE/TIM/SP/35 |
| The Value of Forests: Payments for Ecosystem Services in a Green Economy | ECE/TIM/SP/34 |
| Forest Products Annual Market Review 2012-2013 | ECE/TIM/SP/33 |
| The Lviv Forum on Forests in a Green Economy | ECE/TIM/SP/32 |
| Forests and Economic Development: A Driver for the Green Economy in the ECE Region | ECE/TIM/SP/31 |
| Forest Products Annual Market Review 2011-2012 | ECE/TIM/SP/30 |
| The North American Forest Sector Outlook Study 2006-2030 | ECE/TIM/SP/29 |
| European Forest Sector Outlook Study 2010-2030 | ECE/TIM/SP/28 |
| Forest Products Annual Market Review 2010-2011 | ECE/TIM/SP/27 |
| Private Forest Ownership in Europe | ECE/TIM/SP/26 |
| Forest Products Annual Market Review 2009-2010 | ECE/TIM/SP/25 |
| Forest Products Annual Market Review 2008-2009 | ECE/TIM/SP/24 |
| Forest Products Annual Market Review 2007-2008 | ECE/TIM/SP/23 |
| Forest Products Annual Market Review 2006-2007 | ECE/TIM/SP/22 |
| Forest Products Annual Market Review, 2005-2006 | ECE/TIM/SP/21 |
| European Forest Sector Outlook Study: 1960 – 2000 – 2020, Main Report | ECE/TIM/SP/20 |
| Forest policies and institutions of Europe, 1998-2000 | ECE/TIM/SP/19 |
| Forest and Forest Products Country Profile: Russian Federation | ECE/TIM/SP/18 |
| *(Country profiles also exist on Albania, Armenia, Belarus, Bulgaria, former Czech and Slovak Federal Republic, Estonia, Georgia, Hungary, Lithuania, Poland, Romania, Republic of Moldova, Slovenia and Ukraine)* | |
| Forest resources of Europe, CIS, North America, Australia, Japan and New Zealand | ECE/TIM/SP/17 |

***Note**: Additional market-related information is available in electronic format at* ***www.unece.org/forests**.*

**Geneva Timber and Forest Discussion Papers (original language only)**

| | |
|---|---|
| COVID-19 Impacts on the Forest Sector in Countries in countries in the Western Balkans | *ECE/TIM/DP/89 |
| COVID-19 Impacts on the Forest Sector in Countries in countries Eastern Europe, Caucasus and Central Asia | *ECE/TIM/DP/88 |
| Forest Landscape Restoration in Eastern and South-East Europe | ECE/TIM/DP/87 |
| Overview of the State of Forests and Forest Management in Uzbekistan | ECE/TIM/DP/85 |
| Overview of the State of Forests and Forest Management in Turkmenistan | ECE/TIM/DP/84 |
| Overview of the State of Forests and Forest Management in Tajikistan | ECE/TIM/DP/83 |
| Overview of the State of Forests and Forest Management in Kyrgyzstan | ECE/TIM/DP/82 |
| Overview of the State of Forests and Forest Management in Kazakhstan | ECE/TIM/DP/81 |
| Overview of the State of Forests and Forest Management in Georgia | ECE/TIM/DP/80 |
| Overview of the State of Forests and Forest Management in Azerbaijan | ECE/TIM/DP/79 |
| Overview of the State of Forests and Forest Management in Armenia | ECE/TIM/DP/78 |
| Guidelines on the Promotion of Green Jobs in Forestry | ECE/TIM/DP/77 |
| Forest Sector Workforce in the UNECE Region | ECE/TIM/DP/76 |
| Rovaniemi Action Plan for the Forest Sector in a Green Economy: Mid-term Review | ECE/TIM/DP/75 |
| Trends in green jobs in the forest sector in the UNECE region | ECE/TIM/DP/74 |
| Guidelines for the Development of a Criteria and Indicator Set for Sustainable Forest Management | ECE/TIM/DP/73 |
| Forest Landscape Restoration in the Caucasus and Central Asia | ECE/TIM/DP/72 |
| Green Jobs in the Forest Sector | *ECE/TIM/DP/71 |
| Measuring the Value of Forests in a Green Economy | *ECE/TIM/DP/70 |
| Forecast of the Committee on Forests and the Forest Industry: Forest Products Production and Trade 2016-2018 | *ECE/TIM/DP/69 |
| Forecast of the Committee on Forests and the Forest Industry: Forest Products Production and Trade 2015-2017 | *ECE/TIM/DP/68 |
| ECE Committee on Forests and the Forest Industry and European Forestry Commission: 70 years working in the Service of Forests and people | ECE/TIM/DP/67 |
| Pilot project on the System for the Evaluation of the Management of Forests (SEMAFOR) | ECE/TIM/DP/66 |
| Comparative assessment of wood biomass for energy in Europe | *ECE/TIM/DP/65 |
| Forecast of the Committee on Forests and the Forest Industry: Forest Products Production and Trade 2014-2016 | ECE/TIM/DP/64 |
| Forecast of the Committee on Forests and the Forest Industry: Forest Products Production and Trade 2013-2015 | ECE/TIM/DP/63 |
| Competitiveness of the European Forest Sector | ECE/TIM/DP/62 |
| Forecast of the Committee on Forests and the Forest Industry: Forest Products Production and Trade 2012-2014 | ECE/TIM/DP/61 |
| Forecast of the Committee on Forests and the Forest Industry: Forest Products Production and Trade 2011-2013 | ECE/TIM/DP/60 |
| Econometric Modelling and Projections of Wood Products Demand, Supply and Trade in Europe | ECE/TIM/DP/59 |
| Swedish Forest Sector Outlook Study | ECE/TIM/DP/58 |
| The Importance of China's Forest Products Markets to the UNECE Region | ECE/TIM/DP/57 |
| Good Practice Guidance on Sustainable Mobilisation of Wood: Proceedings from the Grenoble Workshop | *ECE/TIM/DP/56 |
| Harvested Wood Products in the Context of Climate Change Policies: Workshop Proceedings - 2008 | *ECE/TIM/DP/55 |
| The Forest Sector in the Green Economy | ECE/TIM/DP/54 |
| National Wood Resources Balances: Workshop Proceedings | *ECE/TIM/DP/53 |
| Potential Wood Supply in Europe | *ECE/TIM/DP/52 |
| Wood Availability and Demand in Europe | *ECE/TIM/DP/51 |
| Forest Products Conversion Factors for the UNECE Region | ECE/TIM/DP/49 |
| Mobilizing Wood Resources: Can Europe's Forests Satisfy the Increasing Demand for Raw Material and Energy Under Sustainable Forest Management? Workshop Proceedings - January 2007 | *ECE/TIM/DP/48 |
| European Forest Sector Outlook Study: Trends 2000-2005 Compared to the EFSOS Scenarios | ECE/TIM/DP/47 |
| Forest and Forest Products Country Profile; Tajikistan | *ECE/TIM/DP/46 |
| Forest and Forest Products Country Profile: Uzbekistan | ECE/TIM/DP/45 |
| Forest Certification – Do Governments Have a Role? | ECE/TIM/DP/44 |
| International Forest Sector Institutions and Policy Instruments for Europe: A Source Book | ECE/TIM/DP/43 |
| Forests, Wood and Energy: Policy Interactions | ECE/TIM/DP/42 |
| Outlook for the Development of European Forest Resources | ECE/TIM/DP/41 |

| | |
|---|---|
| Forest and Forest Products Country Profile: Serbia and Montenegro | ECE/TIM/DP/40 |
| Forest Certification Update for the UNECE Region, 2003 | ECE/TIM/DP/39 |
| Forest and Forest Products Country Profile: Republic of Bulgaria | ECE/TIM/DP/38 |
| Forest Legislation in Europe: How 23 Countries Approach the Obligation to Reforest, Public Access and Use of Non-Wood Forest Products | ECE/TIM/DP/37 |
| Value-Added Wood Products Markets, 2001-2003 | ECE/TIM/DP/36 |
| Trends in the Tropical Timber Trade, 2002-2003 | ECE/TIM/DP/35 |
| Biological Diversity, Tree Species Composition and Environmental Protection in the Regional FRA-2000 | ECE/TIM/DP/33 |
| Forestry and Forest Products Country Profile: Ukraine | ECE/TIM/DP/32 |
| The Development of European Forest Resources, 1950 To 2000: a Better Information Base | ECE/TIM/DP/31 |
| Modelling and Projections of Forest Products Demand, Supply and Trade in Europe | ECE/TIM/DP/30 |
| Employment Trends and Prospects in the European Forest Sector | ECE/TIM/DP/29 |
| Forestry Cooperation with Countries in Transition | ECE/TIM/DP/28 |
| Russian Federation Forest Sector Outlook Study | ECE/TIM/DP/27 |
| Forest and Forest Products Country Profile: Georgia | ECE/TIM/DP/26 |
| Forest certification update for the UNECE region, summer 2002 | ECE/TIM/DP/25 |
| Forecasts of economic growth in OECD and central and eastern European countries for the period 2000-2040 | ECE/TIM/DP/24 |
| Forest Certification update for the UNECE Region, summer 2001 | ECE/TIM/DP/23 |
| Structural, Compositional and Functional Aspects of Forest Biodiversity in Europe | ECE/TIM/DP/22 |
| Markets for secondary processed wood products, 1990-2000 | ECE/TIM/DP/21 |
| Forest certification update for the UNECE Region, summer 2000 | ECE/TIM/DP/20 |
| Trade and environment issues in the forest and forest products sector | ECE/TIM/DP/19 |
| Multiple use forestry | ECE/TIM/DP/18 |
| Forest certification update for the UNECE Region, summer 1999 | ECE/TIM/DP/17 |
| A summary of "The competitive climate for wood products and paper packaging: the factors causing substitution with emphasis on environmental promotions" | ECE/TIM/DP/16 |
| Recycling, energy and market interactions | ECE/TIM/DP/15 |
| The status of forest certification in the UNECE region | ECE/TIM/DP/14 |
| The role of women on forest properties in Haute-Savoie (France): Initial research | ECE/TIM/DP/13 |
| Interim report on the Implementation of Resolution H3 of the Helsinki Ministerial Conference on the protection of forests in Europe (Results of the second enquiry) | ECE/TIM/DP/12 |
| Manual on acute forest damage | ECE/TIM/DP/7 |

* signifies electronic publication only

***Many of the above publications can be downloaded free of charge at:***

**www.unece.org/forests**

***Publications and subscriptions are available through United Nations Publications Offices as follows:***

Sales and Marketing Section, Room DC2-853
United Nations
2 United Nations Plaza
New York, NY 10017
United States of America
Fax: + 1 212 963 3489

**E-mail: publications@un.org**

**Web site: https://shop.un.org/**

Information Service
United Nations Economic Commission for Europe

Palais des Nations
CH - 1211 Geneva 10, Switzerland
Telephone: +41(0)22 917 12 34
Fax: +41(0)22 917 05 05
E-mail: unece_info@un.org
Website: http://www.unece.org